REYNAL'S WORLD HISTORY OF GREAT SCULPTURE

GREAT SCULPTURE
OF ANCIENT EGYPT

REYNAL'S WORLD HISTORY OF GREAT SCULPTURE

KAZIMIERZ MICHALOWSKI

GREAT SCULPTURE
OF ANCIENT EGYPT

REYNAL & COMPANY
in association with
WILLIAM MORROW AND COMPANY, INC., NEW YORK
1978

This page, right:
Fragment of a cosmetic spoon,
XVIIIth Dynasty (1580–1314 B.C.*).*
Wood; probably from Thebes.
Berlin, Staatliche Museen.

Page 2: The Prince and Count
Nespekashuti, represented as
a scribe,
XXVIth Dynasty (663–525 B.C.*).*
Green schist; from Karnak.
Cairo, Egyptian Museum.

Page 6: Mourning men,
XVIIIth Dynasty (1580–1314 B.C.*).*
Bas-relief, limestone;
from a tomb at Memphis.
Berlin, Staatliche Museen.

REYNAL'S WORLD HISTORY OF GREAT SCULPTURE

Editorial Director
LORENZO CAMUSSO
Scientific Consultant
MIA CINOTTI

GREAT SCULPTURE OF ANCIENT EGYPT

Text
KAZIMIERZ MICHALOWSKI
Translated from the Italian by
ENID KIRCHBERGER
List of works
GEMMA VERCHI
Notes
ANNA CARPI
Picture research
NICOLETTA POLTRI TANUCCI
Layout
GIOVANNI MELADA
Editorial assistant
MICHELE BUZZI
Editorial secretary
ADA JORIO

English language edition copyright © 1978 by Mondadori-Shogakukan
First published in the United States by Reynal and Company, Inc.
Originally published in Italian in 1978 by Arnoldo Mondadori
Editore, Milano under the title EGITTO
Copyright © 1978 by Mondadori-Shogakukan
Photograph copyright © 1978 by Shogakukan Ltd., Tokyo, Japan
Text copyright © 1978 by Mondadori-Shogakukan
Library of Congress Catalog Card Number 78-52014
ISBN 0-688-61201-6
Printed and bound in Italy by Officine Grafiche di Arnoldo
Mondadori Editore, Verona

CONTENTS

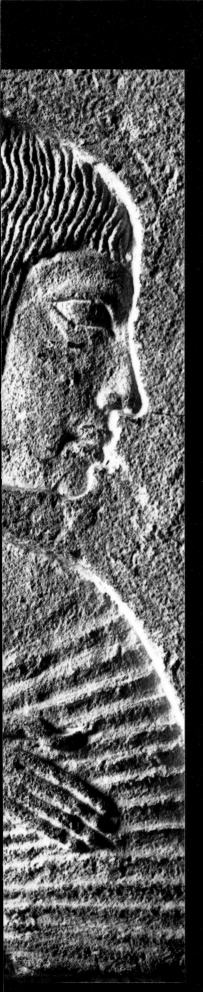

STATUES FOR
THE GOD-KING

O Gods! I am your son, fashioned by your hands.
Within your golden houses I have worked for you
with gold and silver, turquoise and lapis lazuli.
For you I built castles, sanctuaries, cities,
in which your names are carved for all eternity!

—Prayer of Ramesses III to the
Gods upon his accession to the
throne, Twentieth Dynasty. Harris
Papyrus I.

To understand the basic principles underlying the art of the sculptors of ancient Egypt, one usually resorts to a selection of the most representative works of art—which are for that very reason familiar ones. It is obviously impossible to put together a sample group of works that have an absolute value and at the same time illustrate the development of the painting or sculpture of a specific historical period. The process of creation is such a complex phenomenon, and one which, aside from the artist's individuality, is so subject to many other external factors, that the development of a country's art cannot be appreciated through the analysis of a group of works chosen because each is a masterpiece.

First of all, though the artist aspires to reach perfection, he seldom gets even close to his goal. Second, the general artistic output of any given period does not consist only of masterpieces, for these are flanked by minor works that are of lesser importance as far as vitality, expression, artistic value, and quality of workmanship are concerned. But it is important to examine these minor works if we are to understand the process of development of artistic creation in a specific historical period, because it allows us to delve into the manifold functions that art fulfills in society, and above all the function it fulfilled in antiquity.

In this respect, ancient Egypt is not an exception; on the contrary, throughout its history the social function of art was of the highest importance. Independently of the use for which a work of art was destined—religious, funerary, courtly, or, on the other hand, popular—the figurative art of Egypt developed in the course of three thousand years an idiom restricted within general principles. This idiom was reached after several centuries of experiments by artists in the prehistoric and predynastic periods, at about the same time the

political and internal economic and social structures were established—that is, after the unification of Upper and Lower Egypt into a single state with a centralized policy.

The Egyptians arrived at this state of affairs after a long and bloody struggle and many unsuccessful attempts. Yet the geographic and climatic conditions of their country—in which survival depended on the regularity of the flooding of the Nile—were such that there had developed a type of social structure which ensured—at least from the First Cataract of the Nile to its branching off in the Delta—a uniform administration of the country's economy, which consisted mostly of a fixed system of irrigation.

Artistic creation, which was to develop into a very important function of the complex machinery of state, was subjected to a "classical" hierarchical social structure and a uniform administration. Next to the life-giving function of the Nile, the primary factors on which the order of things was based in Pharaonic Egypt were religion and art.

The homogeneous and very particular character of Egyptian art is such that the works of art of ancient Egypt stand out starkly from among those of Mesopotamia, Syria, Asia Minor, Greece, and Rome. This is the result of a process which was about fifteen hundred years in the making, during the prehistoric (and therefore predynastic) period, which began in the Bronze Age, about 4500 B.C.

There are several important examples: amphoras with relief decorations in the shape of human heads or animals, and sometimes vases in the shape of birds, frogs, or hippopotami. This tendency to give a functional object the shape of an animal can also be found in some of the most characteristic predynastic objects discovered during archeological digs: schist tablets (also known as palettes, because they were sometimes used to mix cosmetics), which were found in tombs and places of worship and which often had a purely votive function. The oldest cosmetic tablets are geometric in shape and not decorated, but later they take on animal shapes (that of a tortoise, for instance). At the end of the predynastic period they show figurative relief decorations. Other zoomorphic functional objects were made of bone: broaches adorned with the outline of a bird or a bull's head; combs with figures of antelopes, gazelles, or even of human beings. At the same time objects of copper and gold began to be used; the earliest razors, made of copper; knife handles adorned with gold plate worked in relief with hunts or battle scenes. More zoomorphic inspiration: in the later tombs of that period fragments of wooden furniture were found—small tables, stools, and beds with feet in the shape of bulls' hooves.

Recent archeological expeditions in Nubia have brought to light an interesting and little-known kind of prehistoric art: drawings engraved or hammered out of rock, representing boats and animals. Among them are examples of animals, such as the giraffe, which disappeared from Egypt thousands of years ago.

There are also terra-cotta figurines of women, which probably represent slaves from African tribes. Some of them still show traces of polychrome decoration representing clothes or ritual ornaments. They are characterized by the pronounced shape of the breasts and exaggeratedly large hips, probably a deliberate emphasis of the more significant feminine traits. If we examine one of the most characteristic examples of this type of object, a figurine dating from the fourth millennium, found in a tomb at Marmarica and generally thought to represent a goddess, we should probably be close to the truth if, looking at the shape of the statuette, we consider it an example of the conception of female beauty of the period.

Statuary, which was to play such an important part in the art of ancient Egypt, nevertheless developed rather slowly. We have mentioned the decorations on the stone amphoras and bone objects. Nevertheless, zoomorphic or anthropomorphic stone figures of modest dimensions appear only at the end of the predynastic period. The same can be said of the reliefs on the palettes and knife handles.

The unification of Egypt was, of course, a crucial event in the country's history. The political merging of the southern and northern territories and the resulting social and political restructuring were a salutary event. This was reflected in art. Indeed, a very important change is noticeable in Egyptian art after the unification of Upper and Lower Egypt and the consolidation of the new organism of state in the course of the first two dynasties. The character of this change—essentially a new way of looking at things—which distinguishes the new art from the art of the predynastic period can be appreciated by comparing works of art of the same type—cosmetic palettes, for example.

The most famous of these palettes is the one that belonged to Narmer, whom it is now possible to identify as the Pharaoh Menes, who, according to historical tradition, unified the two territories and founded the First Dynasty. In the predynastic tablets the general impression of the composition is somewhat chaotic; it is difficult at first glance to make out what is represented. An example of this is the "Battlefield Palette," which is shared by the British Museum and the Ashmolean at Oxford. Narmer's large tablet, however (see pp. 13, 175), which was found in Hierakonpolis and is now in the Cairo Museum, marks the beginning of the concept of orderly composition. It is sculpted on both sides and is capped by two animal protomas with curved horns between which is written the king's so-called name of Horus. The front of the tablet is intricately carved but neatly subdivided. It is dominated by the figure of the king, wearing the crown of Upper Egypt and a loincloth, with a long tail fixed to the back of his waist. He is brandishing a mace in his right hand and is about to hit with it a Libyan prisoner of war kneeling at his feet. Above the Libyan the falcon god Horus holds another bearded prisoner by the neck. The six flower-topped stalks stemming from this prisoner's back symbolize the six thousand prisoners of war taken as slaves. Behind the king, on the left, is the small figure of a dignitary holding a vessel in his right hand and a pair of sandals in his left. At the bottom is a separate strip showing two bearded and naked Libyans in the act of fleeing.

The back of the tablet, which is also capped by the two protomas and the king's name, is divided into three horizontal areas. The top part shows the king, the tallest of the figures there. He is shown in the act of walking, wearing the crown of Lower Egypt, holding the mace in his left hand and the *nehaha*, or whip, in his right. The dignitary represented on the front of the tablet—again half the king's size—is walking behind the sovereign; before him, also in a much smaller size, is a minister, as indicated by the hieroglyphics above his head. Ahead of them all walk four standard bearers carrying long standards with the arms of the four *nomoi*, or Egyptian provinces. On the right-hand part of this top area are ten figures of defeated enemies, lying two abreast with their hands tied and their severed heads between their feet. The composition of the scene is remarkably clear and legible. The king is easily recognizable, not only because of his crown but also because he is twice the size of his two dignitaries. In addition, his name—Narmer—is given on the back of the tablet as well as the front

(by his head, between the figure of the minister and the standards). The standard bearers' social position is obviously inferior to that of the minister and this is indicated by their stature, which is even smaller than his. Both the number and the condition of the defeated enemies are evident; they were obviously tied together before they were beheaded.

The middle area represents a rather curious scene: with their long necks two fantastic lion-headed animals form a concave circular area which constitutes the cosmetic palette. The animals are held on a leash by two figures on either side. Two raised lines divide the middle area from the other two; the top line forms the base for the figures on the top part and the lower line the base for the fantastic animals. The lower area of the tablet shows a bull destroying a fortress with its horns and treading on a fallen Libyan (at the time the bull was the symbol of the king).

If we examine the composition and character of the tablet of Narmer, which has just been described in detail, and of the British Museum tablet mentioned earlier, we can easily perceive the change that came over Egyptian art immediately after the unification of Upper and Lower Egypt. Both tablets have a single identical theme: war. In Narmer's tablet, however, war has one precise aim, which is that the unity of the state should be preserved—a state governed by a single king to whose decision every event must be subjected. All ideology and superstructure are subject to a single idea—the glorification of the pharaoh's power. It must therefore be proclaimed throughout the land that a stable order has been achieved which can be preserved as long as everybody's duty is rigidly delimited in relation to the pharaoh's power, which is synonymous with the power of the state. The result of this was the establishment of a social hierarchy and the carefully delimited position of every individual in the country.

Art fulfilled a precise and obvious function in the ideological superstructure of the kingdom. The condition necessary to make it into an efficient instrument for expressing and above all spreading and impressing this ideology into the minds of the people—in other words, the condition necessary to make it into an instrument of propaganda for the state—was that it should be easily understood and found legible by all. It is a fact that a work of art which is clear and explicit can have a power of persuasion that words—and above all coercion—cannot have. Pictures and images settle in the mind and, along with them, what they represent—things, men, events. Thus they give the key to the way in which what they represent—things, men, events—must be viewed and understood. Every one of us notices more than once in his life what power of suggestion certain interpretations—such as the pictorial interpretation—of historical events can have, and how these events are assimilated culturally through the medium of a work of art.

In fact Narmer's tablet was a courtly object, probably of a votive nature, and therefore it is most unlikely that it was seen by a large number of people. Nevertheless, the ideology underlying the new artistic expression is already evident in it. Later this new art was to address itself to the whole of society from the walls of temples and tombs.

Having sketched the aim of this new form of expression, we can now examine the means through which it achieved its results: what made this art accessible, comprehensible, legible to all? In the predynastic tablets the accessibility of the message was impaired by the confused, chaotic composition, so that it was difficult to know where to start looking in order to understand the message. In Narmer's tablet, on the other hand, the various

scenes are set in different areas. The link between the hieroglyphic inscriptions and the division of the areas is quite clear. So it is obvious that the scenes must be deciphered according to each area, in the same way each of the individual pictograms of the hieroglyphic writing could be deciphered by those who could read them.

The use of the larger size for important characters is both an early and an efficient convention. Today the idea of arranging the figures of the tied and beheaded enemies one above the other may seem naïve—realistically a scene like the one in Narmer's tablet should have shown the figures one behind the other—but we have to admit that the way the artist chose to depict these figures has the merit of expressing quite clearly what he wanted to express. At that time only a depiction of reality devoid of any allusions and suggestive devices could be accessible. Reality had to be shown. The artist had the problem of showing things not as he could see them but as he in fact knew they were. This leads us to the problem of perspective. It is not true to say that the Egyptians did not apply the use of perspective; in fact their representation on a three-dimensional plane follows a type of inverted or "reprojected" perspective—what recent research defines as "aspective," the opposite of perspective proper. Nevertheless, the Egyptian way of drawing was close to the principles of technical drawing, and there too certain simplified conventions were developed and adopted.

We have seen how, once the political unification of Upper and Lower Egypt was achieved, between the end of the fourth and the beginning of the third millennium B.C., the art of ancient Egypt aimed at spreading to the people the image of a new, stabler society and the glory of the pharaoh and the gods. A composition divided into areas or strips and the use of the so-called aspective type of perspective made it more accessible and easy to understand. But these were not the only elements that made it successful as a means of propaganda and that helped to establish the particular style which remained basically unchanged for thousands of years. The most important achievement of Egyptian figurative art was the elaboration of the rules concerning the representation of the human figure.

This was not really a discovery and even less the adoption of revolutionary norms. What we call "the canon of Egyptian sculpture" is the result of a process that took a long time to evolve.

Just as the unification of the two lands came about only after many attempts, so the establishment of the norms for the canon was a process that can be traced from its earliest manifestations right up to its classical form. And it is important here to make a distinction between the two different ways of representing the human figure. On the one hand we have three-dimensional sculpture that reproduces something from nature, as in statuary, sculpture in the round. On the other we have three-dimensional objects transferred onto a flat surface, as in the human figure in painting and relief. The canon applies different solutions to these.

The first solution concerns the gods and the ruling class—that is, the kings and the higher dignitaries (which sometimes included only those of royal blood). For all these a particular convention was imposed by the canon. In painting, relief, and statuary, those belonging to the ruling class were shown in "hieratic" attitudes, seated or in the act of walking. These were the attitudes in which the public saw them and it was difficult for his subjects to imagine the king, for example, in any other attitude, for he was never seen at close quarters. The king was god, the living embodiment of Horus. It was not strange, therefore, that his divine body should be shown to be imbued with "timeless

the eye, the torso & the legs

Votive tablet of Pharaoh Narmer,
Ist Dynasty (c. 3000 B.C.).
Cairo, Egyptian Museum.

13

youth." Because none of his subjects could look closely at the king, no one could know what his distinguishing traits were or discover any imperfections in his anatomy. Besides, his chest was almost always covered by a wide, heavy pectoral. His features, on the other hand, were in a sense known to all, for there were effigies and portrait-statues of the king in every temple. These were obviously "official" portraits, portraits in which the king's face was depicted without any indication of feeling or mood. This has been the basic characteristic of all official portraiture up to the present; one cannot help thinking of Queen Elizabeth II's official portraits. Faced with the problems posed by an official portrait, the artist's attitude is not to analyze but to synthesize: he simplifies and synthesizes the features. For this reason, in Egyptian portraits of the Old Kingdom we have "synthesized portraits" of the pharaoh and dignitaries.

Here are a few examples: King Chephren, in a diorite statue (pp. 34, 89), is shown enthroned, with Horus surrounding the *klaft*, or linen head-dress, with his wings; the king's hands are placed on his thighs. The second position stipulated by the Old Kingdom canon can be seen in the statue of Mycerinus (p. 90), in which the pharaoh is shown walking, with his arms hanging down along his body and his fists closed. His face is "timelessly young," and he is wearing the crown of Upper Egypt. The pharaoh stands between the goddess Hathor and a female figure symbolizing the *nomos* (province) of Cynopolis. Like the statue of Chephren, this is an example of "synthesized" portraiture. Another pharaoh of the Old Kingdom, Pepy I (p. 93), and his son Merenra were portrayed in two statues (a larger and a smaller one), which are now in the Cairo Museum. These are made of thin sheets of copper covering a wooden base onto which they are nailed with copper nails (metal

casting was known to artists of the Old Kingdom, but it was used only for smaller figures).

Further examples of this type of sculpture at this period can be found in two other statues in polychrome limestone, also in the Cairo Museum, the statue of Prince Rahotep and of his wife Nofret (pp. 36, 94, 95). The male statue's skin is painted a dark brick-red and the female statue's yellow.

If the pharaoh and higher dignitaries were unreachable and invisible, this was not the case for the second social grade, the officials, whose functions in the social structure of ancient Egypt were mostly of an executive nature. The officials were important people but could nevertheless have been seen at close quarters by the people. Even a nomarch, or governor of a province, could sometimes be approached with a petition by the poorest peasant; as for the head of a village, he was constantly surrounded by the humbler people. The characteristic traits of these officials being well known to all, including their constitutions and any anatomical defects, it was therefore reasonable that for that second social grade the canon should prescribe elements relating to their role. The hieratic attitudes, sitting and walking, were used; for rendering the face and body, however, "timeless youth" was not advocated, but rather a realism that brought out the person's individuality.

An excellent example of this type of sculpture is the "Sheikh el Beled," which means in Arabic "head of the village" (p. 37). He is shown in one of the two hieratic positions proper to an official, but the man himself is corpulent, with fat cheeks and a distended belly. Here we find two very different uses of artistic language in the depiction of characters from the first and second social grades, between the pharaoh and those who executed his orders: for the former, "timeless youth"; for the latter, realism in the representation of their faces and bodies.

14

As we know, the scribe—the public writer—had a very important place in Egyptian society. Although he did not exercise any power (unless he was a head scribe), his profession nevertheless placed him in the second social grade. On the other hand, his activity could in a sense be considered manual labour, which put him near the third social grade. This ambiguity is reflected in art. In a relief in the tomb of Hesyra, at Saqqara, Hesyra is depicted in the walking hieratic position; he holds in his hand a scribe's tools, denoting his function, but because he was a scribe who had achieved a certain responsibility, he is also shown holding a kind of scepter in his right hand, and in his left, together with the inkwell and other writing instruments, is a long staff. In statuary the artist's treatment of the scribe is quite different; he is shown seated, with his legs folded under him and a papyrus roll on his knees. This pose can be seen, for instance, in a famous statue of the Fifth Dynasty (p. 38), showing the scribe at work. The form of the composition, first devised to represent a dignitary, now serves to depict a scribe, but in fact the scribe in this position belongs to the third social grade, which comprises those who work with their hands.

The importance of the scribe's function in Egyptian society is counterproved in his role in art: the seated figure of the scribe becomes a model form in its own right, developing a kind of autonomous canon which in time leads to a cubic form, covered with inscriptions, from which only the head emerges. This model first appears towards the end of the Fifth Dynasty, spreads during the Middle Kingdom period, and reaches its height with a partly abstract cubic form during the New Kingdom period. The later cubic shape of the figure may have a religious reason.

Although the general rules evolved for the representation of the human figure had to be respected, representation of manual workers, the third social grade, was not subject to rigid rules for positions or attitudes. As for all actions, the act of working had to be represented in such a way that the activity depicted was evident and legible. The worker himself was, of course, of lesser importance than the activity he was engaged in. The mastabas of the Fourth and Fifth dynasties at Saqqara are filled with magnificent reliefs showing hosts of peasants, reapers, shepherds, and craftsmen at work in fields, farms, warehouses, shops; fishermen fishing, carpenters building boats, and also musicians and dancers. They represent an extraordinary document of the life of the people in ancient Egypt. If we examine carefully the figures of these workers intent upon so many different tasks and depicted in so many different attitudes, we see that the rigid principle of the frontal depiction of the shoulders is not as restrictive to the artist as it may seem, and that the expressive power and deep realism of these reliefs are probably due to the freedom the artist enjoyed in depicting the human body. The figure of the workman bending under the load of papyrus on his shoulders clearly has a great capacity to move the onlooker.

There is also a series of sculptures—painted limestone statuettes—representing various domestic activities: for example, a woman grinding corn (p.113), another woman making beer (p. 110). They are realistic little figures in which the artist caught the movement beautifully. In the past these domestic scenes were labelled "minor works of sculpture" as opposed to the "major works of sculpture" representing officials, gods, and pharaohs. In many ways this differentiation is unfair. For one thing, even the "major" works were sometimes very small. Nor is the great line dividing official sculpture from the rest valid. If this were so, in which category would one place the "Sheikh el

Beled," that majestic, smiling wooden masterpiece? Furthermore, rigorously official reliefs are full of everyday scenes: crowds of servants bent double under the weight of sacrificial victims in temple reliefs, products brought back from the expedition to the land of Punt, as in the temple of Queen Hatshepsut at Deir el Bahri. The criterion of subject matter may sometimes be used to establish certain distinctions, but certain subjects (battle scenes, landscapes, still-lifes, and so on) cannot be classified separately from the rest of art. The basic element will always be the type and character of the composition, all the more so in Egyptian art, in which form is always closely linked to a determined social content.

The different rules governing the representation of the human figure according to social grades can be seen in the relief representing the official Ti in a boat among his servants (p. 180). The main character, noticeably taller than the other figures and shown in a hieratic position, is depicted according to the rules of the canon. The others, shown in different attitudes according to what they are doing, give the scene its expression as far as both content and form are concerned.

The realism of Egyptian art is purely indigenous, and as such it is a phenomenon that cannot be copied. It is a brand of realism that reflects the particular character of the country, which was linked, for a long time, to an unchanging rhythm in its daily working activity: insignificant technical progress; a religion which was incomprehensible to other peoples; dress, instruments, and tools virtually unchanged for thousands of years; a relatively high level of culture reached rather rapidly but no progress afterwards; the Nile regulating all life, and holding even the gods in its sway.

For the Egyptians everything in their art was entirely clear and easy to understand; this is not always true for us, from where we now look at it. Plato himself noticed and was amazed at the rigidity and simplification of certain forms, and we tend to agree with him. No artist, says Plato, who had been commissioned to sculpt a figure was allowed to stray away from traditional rules, not even in the tiniest detail. This rigidity was perfectly coherent with the conditions of life at the time. Art had evolved rules that answered the needs of the period and that were the guarantee of the art's legibility, a legibility that in turn allowed it to address itself directly to the mass of the people.

Naturalism and realism are two aesthetic categories; today we are able to make a distinction between them. In naturalism the artist catches and fixes a chance instant in the world around us according to his individual vision. Realism has a more general meaning: it is an attempt to represent a phenomenon in a typical form, a phenomenon caught and fixed in art in such a way as to be invested with a general meaning that can be perceived and understood by whoever looks at it. And in this sense Egyptian art was realistic art.

We have examined the active function of art in the ideological superstructure of the state. A systematic structure is implicit in that function. Moreover, the use of such a structure corresponded rather well with the way of life—in which individuality was given little emphasis—of the ancient Egyptians. The king and the priests maintained rigorously determined attitudes before the people, but human labour too was governed in practice by rigidly defined gestures and movements. The representation in art of, for instance, an Egyptian carpenter busy cutting wood, or a butcher slaughtering animals, is restricted to a few basic gestures observed by the artist. Even today if we look at a factory worker we notice that his movements are limited in number and constantly repeated. Two other factors complete the picture: the typical (and to our taste somewhat theatrical) use of gesture of Oriental peoples; and the high degree of specialization in each field of activity.

If we take these points into account, it is not difficult to understand that in depicting certain scenes the artist availed himself of predetermined schemes of composition. Repetition is inevitable if the artist is to remain faithful to the scheme, but it does not mean that the scheme remains unchanged forever and in every period. In fact the scheme of composition of a scene representing woodcutters is different in the Old Kingdom from what it is in the Middle Kingdom.

We have so far discussed the "canon" in Old Kingdom sculpture. This may be summarized into five basic points:

1. The canon is a historically conditioned element of indigenous character.
2. It is the result of a mass of observations and experiences that lead to the fixing in art of the most typical forms found in nature but brought down to specific and constant proportions.
3. Its aim is to depict in the most "legible and comprehensible" idiom and to reflect reality not only as a visible but also as a social experience.
4. It fulfills an active function in the ideological superstructure, which serves the ruling class, by reinforcing the conviction that the social order is stable and just through the glorification of the gods and the king.
5. It is one of the essential conditions for creating teamwork in workshops, to maintain a high level of production and quality.

Towards the end of the Sixth Dynasty Egypt experienced an upheaval that may have started as a palace revolution but soon developed into a social revolution. The nomarchs were at war among themselves and as a result the unity of the state disintegrated and the population found itself generally impoverished. We gather from various texts that there were attempts at organizing a kind of collective power extending over the entire territory—something perhaps similar to a central committee, as the Dutch Egyptologist Adolf Klaesens remarked recently—which would keep the power of the state intact. Whatever the precise events, it is certain that a partial "democratization" of funeral rites can be noticed at this period. It was no longer only the pharaoh or the higher officials who had the right to become Osiris in person after death, but anyone whose family could afford to offer him the prescribed funeral rites. The poorest labourer could now afford to have in his tomb the terra-cotta statuette of a naked woman who would be his concubine after death and would also help him with his work.

As far as sculpture at that period is concerned, it can be noticed that the proportions of the human figure on funerary stelae are no longer rigidly faithful to the old minutely elaborated rules: sometimes the head is too large, the eye or the hand holding a vessel too elongated. This slackening in the rules of composition goes hand in hand with a decline in the quality of the workmanship. The so-called models are among the most characteristic works of that period. The word model is in fact misleading, for they are groups of painted wooden figures of smallish dimensions which were placed in princes' tombs. Among them the troops of armed, marching soldiers stand out (pp. 44, 115).

Another radical change that affected Egyptian art came when the Theban princes succeeded in unifying the country once again. Two new dynasties were founded in Thebes, the Eleventh and the Twelfth. We are now in the Middle Kingdom period, when all the kings looked back at the past and the great Memphite dynasties—in particular at the powerful kings of the Fourth and Fifth dynasties whom they tried to imitate in all things. The economic basis of kingly power, however, was considerably less healthy than it had been in the Old Kingdom.

In art there were several formal innovations. It was during the Middle Kingdom period, for instance, that a new type of capital appeared which differed from its predecessors with their stylized motifs of palm, papyrus, or lotus leaves. The new capital sported on both sides the head of the goddess Hathor. As the "Hathorian capital" it was to be one of the mainstays of Egyptian architecture for a long time. Another innovation was the "Osirian column," although it is likely that similar columns had already been used in the lower parts of temples in the Old Kingdom. The Osirian column consisted of the effigy of the god Osiris resting on a quadrangular pilaster. Also new to this period were the granite sphinxes placed before the portals of the great temple compounds, together with two slender obelisks carved from a single block of red granite and covered with inscriptions. The points of the obelisks were sometimes overlaid with shiny precious metals.

During the Eleventh Dynasty, at the beginning of the Middle Kingdom, there were two different schools or production centers of sculpture. In the north the artists who had to meet the orders issued by the new sovereigns could get their inspiration from the magnificent Old Kingdom monuments and reliefs preserved in the great necropolises around Memphis (Giza, Abu Sir, Saqqara). As a result the sculptures of this northern school have better proportions and a finer finish. The case was different for the south, where there were neither great works of sculpture dating back to the Old Kingdom nor local traditions that might have helped artists reach a high level of workmanship. This is why a certain naïve treatment of facial expression and a general crudeness in execution can be seen in the monument to Nebhepetra Mentuhotpe (p. 47).

At the beginning of the Twelfth Dynasty, however, Egyptian art recovered a certain unity of style, and artists' workshops reached a relatively high degree of competence. Harking back to Old Kingdom values was only a passing phase, but one of its results was greater care lavished on details: the hieroglyphics, for instance, seem more carefully sculpted than in the Old Kingdom. The same may be said of the bas-reliefs, especially the prevailing "hollowed-out" type. The emblem of the reunification of Upper and Lower Egypt is in evidence in all official art: a spinal column linking together the lotus and the papyrus, the plants symbolizing the two territories. Some of the new subject matter would have been unthinkable in the Old Kingdom. We see, for instance, Senwosret I in the last leg of his ritual race before the image of Min, while previously the figures of the king and the deity were treated on a par.

If one tries to examine the way the monuments of this period differ from those of the Old Kingdom, one may come to the conclusion that what is missing in them is the sense of majestic perfection and supreme sereneness that the older monuments possessed—the impression they give of being unchangeable and eternal in a constantly changing and transient world. King Hor, probably the next to last pharaoh of the Twelfth Dynasty, agreed to be portrayed naked but wearing the ceremonial wig and false beard, and with the symbolic *ka*, his "double," or spiritual personality—consisting of a pair of arms opened wide—on the top of his head (p. 128). In the same vein we have the medium-size polychrome wood portrait of King Senwosret I wearing the crown of Lower Egypt (p. 116). It looks as though the Middle Kingdom sculptors no longer had the conviction that they were part of an unchanging and eternal world and that they were therefore called upon to create indestructible works. This was not at all strange. Gone were the days of Cheops, Chephren, and Mycerinus; recent memories were only of wars, revolutions, famine, the decay of the state and of ancient values.

A pessimistic vein runs through the literature of that time, and some historians have tried to see the same phenomenon in art; but here the situation is more complex. There are portraits like those of Amenemhat II and Senwosret III, the most famous kings of the Twelfth Dynasty, which may lead one to think that the rigid principles of the synthesized portrait were finally abandoned; they have lined faces, deep-set eyes, heavy eyelids, sad faces with melancholy, disillusioned eyes. When we remember the portraits of Chephren or Mycerinus the gap appears to be immense. These are not isolated cases, but rather a type of pharaonic portrait which has its counterpart in statues, particularly those of Senwosret III. The mournful face of the king—one would almost say it expresses awareness of the instability of his newly unified state and the obstacles encountered in the daily exercise of power—seems to have become a type of portrait of the "pessimistic king," probably born from observation of an individual's features but soon becoming a new stylistic form, a new convention.

Those "pessimistic" portraits of Amenemhat II and Senwosret III (p. 119) are probably the high point of Middle Kingdom art. Apart from a few sporadic attempts by some sculptors to break the rigid conventions of the traditional system, the rest of the statuary of that time is imbued with a cold and sometimes even banal academic classicism.

This is evident in the statuettes of officials (with their exaggeratedly large and protruding ears) and the "genre" statuettes—such as the figure of a woman nursing a child—which might have merited a more inventive treatment. Faithfully respecting the convention, the artists of the period seem to have intentionally avoided greater freedom of expression.

Egypt was soon steeped in tragedy once more, this time the struggle against the Hyksos invaders. Once again there was discord, internal warfare, and the disintegration of the state. But in fact the Hyksos kings, during the period of their domination in the Delta, had no intention of destroying Egypt's past. The fact that they sometimes had their own names inscribed on Middle Kingdom monuments may point to the contrary, but nevertheless they did not impart a dynamic impulse to art and culture. During the Hyksos reign Egyptian history knew a second period of transition, which perhaps did not cause as much damage as the first, but which nevertheless stopped, or at least slowed down, any possibility of further development for about two centuries.

An enormous change took place, however, in the next period, that of the New Kingdom. Even if we had no other evidence to sustain it, the very quantity of works of art that have survived point to the fact that this was a period of maximum political, military, and economic power and of great cultural and artistic flowering: victorious campaigns against Egypt's enemies, rich booty, a solid economy, and a wealthy society. Large sections of the population began to benefit from a relatively high standard of living. This is evidenced by the series of portraits of architects and scribes; by the decoration of the tombs of craftsmen and stonecutters; by the funerary stelae of ordinary people, placed away from the burial sites in the compound of Osiris at Abydos—an artistic patrimony that adds to and modifies the picture suggested by the great granite statues and the reliefs on temple walls glorifying the pharaoh and the gods. The life of the Egyptian workers improved with the employment of masses of prisoners of war in agriculture and also probably in public works. Slaves were used even in the administration of temples. Where the general improvement of living conditions was probably less felt was in the case of the peasant, the *fellah*, whose life was forever tied to the eternal cycle of harvests and the flooding of the Nile.

Although nothing was changed in the social hierarchy, there was greater opportunity for social advancement than in the past. There are some significant examples: the fate and career of the architect Senmut, for instance, who was the lover of Queen Hatshepsut and was put in charge of her children's education; or the privilege obtained from King Amenhotpe III by another architect, Amenhotpe son of Hapy, to have a funerary temple built for his *ka*. This extraordinary event raised a common mortal to almost the same level as a king.

Archeology has shown that in this period the possession of precious objects was no longer confined to the circle of the king and the ruling class. This development is also found among Asiatic populations with whom the Egyptians at that time had frequent commercial relations and were often at war. The decorative arts continued the tradition of the Old and Middle Kingdom, but in the New Kingdom they reached the remarkable level achieved by the objects found in Tutankhamun's tomb. Elegantly made objects of metal, stone, or wood (p. 4), genuine small masterpieces, were also found in the tombs of ordinary craftsmen of the time.

Functional objects—toilet accessories, orna-ments, clothes—were all distinguished by a remarkable elegance and refinement, and the same atmosphere can be found in painting and sculpture. The human figure becomes more slender, full of lightness and grace. In their drawing and modelling artists reveal a search for beauty which tones down the rigour of the canon and submits it to the expression of the artist's individuality. During the reign of Thutmose III, in the tomb of a minister called Rekhmara, a painter was so bold as to depict a female slave from the back. Once upon a time Ptahhotep, a minister of the Fifth Dynasty, had included in his collection of maxims the following: "Art knows no frontiers, but no artist will ever reach perfection." If the second part of this aphorism can be applied to Old Kingdom art, the first part, with its implicit allusion to the freedom of creation, fits beautifully the quite different atmosphere of the New Kingdom.

Among the masterpieces of that period are the bas-reliefs of the early pharaohs of the Eighteenth Dynasty—those of the temple of Queen Hatshepsut at Deir el Bahri and the monuments discovered by the Polish archeological mission in 1962–68, which came from the temple of Thutmose III in the same valley. These are all characterized by a faithful adherence to the norms of the classical canon in both composition and the outline of the human figure. The reliefs of the temple of Thutmose III have kept their colours intact (p. 24); and in Queen Hatshepsut's temple one of the most beautiful reliefs represents a scene with a boat in which the slaves rowing have a dark brown skin, which indicates that they were Nubians.

At some point in the Eighteenth Dynasty there emerged a new technical device which imparted a kind of graceful melancholy to faces. The generation of sculptors of the reliefs in the temples of Hatshepsut and Thutmose III used to outline the eyebrows and the eyelids with a bold stroke. Now, however, the eye was modelled so softly that its surface seemed to merge with the rest of the face. The effect is similar to the *sfumato* of the later marble statues of the school of Alexandria. This more delicate rendering of the eye continued to be applied in some works of the later Eighteenth Dynasty, during the reigns of Tutankhamun and Haremhab.

The greatest king of the Eighteenth Dynasty was Amenhotpe III, and it was during his reign that New Kingdom art reached its apogee. Both in plastic arts and in architecture, classicism, which was present from the very beginning of that period, achieves its most nearly perfect form. This was a general characteristic. It was not restricted to the official art of temple walls and royal tombs; there was in art a moment of unequalled harmony in which the outlines were graceful and subtle and the details full of delicacy and precision. The finest examples of so-called flat relief can be found in the tomb of Ramose, minister and governor of Thebes at the time of Amenhotpe III and IV. In them the hieratic position of the dead man stipulated by the canon is respected, but the face is soft and delicate and the tiniest detail, down to every lock of hair, is rendered with remarkable precision.

There were two contrasting artistic currents in Egyptian art at that time. The first, faithful to the ancient principle of symmetry, projects clearly the objects on the field, pursues the aim of absolute legibility of the image; it is the "conservative" current, and the funerary procession depicted in the tomb of Ramose is an example of it. But on another wall of the same tomb can be seen the expressive gestures of the mourners in their transparent clothes, and the delightful lithe figure of a naked girl. These are examples of the other current, the "progressive" current, which aimed at achieving the fullest expression of content in a concise figurative composition.

The art of the time of Amenhotpe III represents a high point in the history of Egyptian art. It is, however, generally true that the very fact of reaching a moment of perfection in creative expression conceals the trap of academic repetition. The only thing that can save art from falling into academism and rigidity is a new style of expression which can avail itself of the technical know-how achieved so far and transform it into something different with a new content. And this is indeed what happened at this stage in the history of Egyptian art. A profoundly revolutionary change came about with the development of Amarnian art, a unique and original style that was completely different from anything in Egyptian art up to then. And it happened despite the centuries old, petrified principles of the canon which emprisoned artists within its iron discipline. It is not easy for us today to appreciate how difficult it was for Egyptian artists to overrule the canon and to overcome rules which had been consecrated by tradition for the depiction of gods and rituals. It is therefore not surprising that this rejection of the accepted tradition should have occurred at the same time as the "heresy" of Amenhotpe IV, who withdrew from Thebes, which was at that time heavily dominated by the growing power of the priests of Amun at Karnak. It is not true to say, as has been said in the past, that this was due to a real conflict between the king and the priests. What was probably the most important thing for Akhenaton (the new name of Amenhotpe IV) was to found a new seat of power which was not already impregnated with religious and artistic traditions, and in which he could worship the god Aton. The king therefore transferred his residence to a newly founded capital, Akhetaton, on the edge of the desert, close to the present-day village of Tell el 'Amarna.

Having severed all links with tradition, Akhenaton had a new temple built for the worship of a single god, Aton (not to be confused with Atum). A poet in his own right, Akhenaton also undertook to liberate art from its secular bonds. And indeed the art of Akhenaton's time, which drew its inspiration from the king's personal concepts, is a splendid and exceptional—if short-lived—episode in the annals of Egyptian art. If we bear in mind the spirit and conditions underlying the historical development of the art of ancient Egypt up to the time of Akhenaton, we can readily understand how difficult it must have been for artists to put the king's concepts into practice. Akhenaton had issued instructions which were as simple as they were confusing: artists must represent what they see, without idealizing the figure of the king and making his effigies a glorification of royalty. And indeed the king was depicted in art as he was in reality. Once the limits of "official" portraiture were superseded, the artists represented him in intimate moments of his everyday life—in the midst of a gesture of affection towards his wife, playing with his children, or distributing presents to his subjects. When one thinks of how limited artists formerly were in their choice of subject matter, but also how secure in the fact that they were following well-trodden paths, it is easy to see the difficulties and risks involved in this new style, in which both content and form were totally different. In a sense the success of the artists' attempt is the measure of the technical perfection which the Egyptian artists' workshops had reached. Indeed, the artists who were able to make possible the king's artistic program were those he had taken with him from Thebes to his new capital. Archeological excavations at Tell el 'Amarna have brought to light the workshop of a sculptor called Thutmes, in which were found studies for a portrait

of the beautiful Queen Nafertiti (p. 54) who is, with Queen Hatshepsut, the most famous female personality of the New Kingdom. The new spirit of the time was quick to find a concrete form in a series of monuments by Amarnian artists. The large sculptures of Akhenaton are no longer examples of "synthesized" portraits, clothing him in "timeless youth"; instead they show him as he was, with all his physical infelicities: an oval head, with a long, almost horsy jaw, a thin neck, slender, sloping shoulders, and a pot belly. (He was also a brilliantly clever man, since he was able to do away with thousands of years of customs, prejudices, and conventions deeply embedded in the society of his time, and was also able and courageous in his opposition to the power of the priests and other dignitaries.) In bas-relief and painting the scenes of courtly life that fix intimate moments for eternity are among the greatest masterpieces of the time: the king and queen enthroned and surrounded by the little princesses, the little girl eating roast duck (p. 185), two little naked princesses lolling about on cushions in their apartment in the palace.

One such relief represents the king's brother, Smenkhara, with his lover, or spouse, who is proffering a bunch of flowers for him to smell (p. 146). It is interesting to note that Akhenaton's anatomical characteristics, or rather weaknesses—the egg-shaped head, long jaw, and pot belly—are also present in his brother and his brother's wife. It is possible, though not certain, that Smenkhara did indeed have the same physical characteristics as his elder brother, and that these were shared by his consort, who was also his niece, Akhenaton's daughter; but this has not been proved.

In actuality the reason for this "family resemblance," which is shared by all the other characters in the art of that period, may not lie in the mere fact that they were blood relatives. Let us examine, for instance, other sculptures of the time, such as a scene in which slaves are shown carrying offerings or sacrificial victims. Even the slaves have egg-shaped heads. We have reached here the crux of the matter, which is that the habit and need for a canon was so deeply embedded in Egyptian artists that once they had changed the type of royal image to conform with the new concept of realism, the characteristic elements of the king's rather unfortunate figure became the basis for another canon on which all other figures were modelled. And this new canon was the sign of a certain mannerism which eventually submerged Amarnian art.

It is not difficult to accept that a king's immediate circle should be the subject of imitation in matters of clothes, tastes, and gestures. There is a vast number of examples from all periods in history (right up to the Prince of Wales, Edward VIII, who was the arbiter of male elegance for England and other nations too). But one can understand how the artistic rendering of the human figure can be modelled on a king's peculiar anatomy only if one can enter an Egyptian artist's mental sphere and appreciate his tendency, born out of hundreds of years of habit, to depict the human figure according to the stipulations of a canon. That is how this brief moment of glory in the history of Egyptian art, which began with a new, fresh, and salutary effort to supersede the old canon, very rapidly became immersed in mannerism.

The Amarnian style died with the death of Akhenaton/Amenhotpe IV, and artists returned to ancient traditions. We know very little about Smenkhara who reigned for less than three years, perhaps as a co-regent; but funerary articles and paintings from the tomb of Tutankhamun indicate that the final victory was won by the priests of the Theban god Amun, and that art went back to the ancient norms of the traditional canon. The monuments raised during the heretical king's reign were not destroyed immediately after Akhenaton's death, but much later, during the Ramessid period. This fact seems to indicate that the "heresy" was not a violent political and religious happening but rather a pacific event.

The artistic forms created by Amarnian artists were not entirely lost, however. Something of them remained and brought a breath of fresh air to the ancient tradition which once again prevailed. It is evident above all in the treatment of drapery, which became more fluid and softer, after the naturalistic Amarnian treatment, in the art of the time of Tutankhamun (pp. 57–60, 148–149) and of his successors.

The famous polychrome head of Nafertiti (p. 53), now in West Berlin, is one of the last works of the Tell el 'Amarna workshops. It was discovered by German archeologists just before the First World War in the workshop of the sculptor Thutmes. It is made of limestone covered with stucco and is most probably a portrait of the queen which served as a model for other portraits in stone. The head is that of a woman no longer very young, with a long, elegant neck and a crown whose function may have been to hide the oval shape of the typical Amarnian skull. The face is remarkably delicate and the protruding Amarnian jaw is fortunately not in evidence.

The last king of the Eighteenth Dynasty was General Haremhab (p. 78). In his time the norms of the ancient canon were already reestablished and the subject matter once more consisted of ritual processions and sacrifices to the gods. The Amarnian episode was closed but it is not difficult to detect that something of it stayed on, even with the return to ancient tradition: movements are lighter, gestures more deliberately executed; there is a certain affectation and theatricality. The king's

Pharaoh Thutmose III *(1504–1450* B.C.*), XVIIIth Dynasty. Temple of Deir el Bahri.*

hands, as he performs the sacrifice, seem to barely touch the objects they are holding. The rendering of details is rather refined. On a technical plane it is interesting that the habit—dating from the Tell el 'Amarna days—of rendering the toes obliquely (showing the outside) appears quite frequently, even if the ancient way of modelling toes never completely disappears.

During the reign of Sety I, the second pharaoh of the Nineteenth Dynasty, there are fine works of art which fit perfectly within the "academism" that characterized the post-Amarnian period in Egyptian art. There are, for example, bas-reliefs of the pharaoh offering a sacrifice to Isis or Osiris in the temple of Abydos. These "official" scenes of worship, which are in a superb state of preservation, are also interesting because they show the development of the depiction of the king-god relationship. During the Old Kingdom the king spoke to the gods as their equal; during the Middle Kingdom the king is shown performing the ritual "race," or dancing before the gods. Now, however, the king is shown kneeling or even prostrated in the act of complete submission, as we can see with Ramesses II. In this particular case some scholars have theorized that the pharaoh's attitude may have been due to the artist's desire to make the sculpture more static in relation to its base, but this kind of interpretation is unacceptable in view of the narrow margin of maneuver allotted to Egyptian artists. It is the expression of an idea rather than the technical solution of a composition problem.

The basalt statue of Ramesses II enthroned—now in the Turin Museum (p. 156)—shows the king dressed in light, almost transparent clothes; his features are very delicate, faintly Semitic, with a slightly hooked nose. It is not the only example of a softer portrait of a New Kingdom pharaoh, a departure from the harder and rougher portraits of

Old Kingdom kings. There may also have been a social-ethnic difference, for the faces of Chephren and Mycerinus are those of peasants, whereas the New Kingdom kings and princes seem to have been more delicate and aristocratic-looking individuals. There had been many marriages with Hittite and Mitanni princesses, and the addition of Oriental blood must have helped to alter the physical type of the ruling families.

In the Ramessid period Egypt was in a situation that bore a direct relation to the conditions of artistic production. It was a period of much building—in fact a period of excessive and hurried building, so much so that stonecutters, sculptors, and painters could not keep pace, as far as quality was concerned, with the great number of temples ordered by the pharaohs, above all by Ramesses II and Ramesses III. There are signs of mass production in the greater number of works, which were also marked by a general tendency toward decorative motifs. This "decorative" trend can also be seen in the few works distinguished by their delicacy and fine workmanship.

What is perhaps the most interesting example of New Kingdom religious sculpture and architecture was much in the news a few years ago. As we know, the great rock temple of Ramesses II at Abu Simbel (pp. 160–161) no longer stands exactly where it stood originally. It is in Nubia, north of the Second Cataract and not far from the present-day frontier with the Sudan. This temple was threatened with submersion after the building of the Aswan Dam, and after examining a large number of projects for saving the monument, the Egyptian government and UNESCO finally gave their approval to a Swedish project which proposed to cut out the temple of Ramesses and that of Nafertari from the rock by lifting away thirty-ton blocks. The cost of the project was about forty million dollars. The

blocks, transported to the top of the rocky hill, about sixty meters higher than the original emplacement, were reassembled and the temples were rebuilt.

The temple of Ramesses II had been built into the rose-coloured sandstone to celebrate the thirtieth anniversary of his reign. The huge trapezoidal façade, reminiscent of a characteristic element of Egyptian temple structures, the so-called pylon—is decorated by four twenty-meter statues of the king enthroned; at their feet are smaller statues of members of his family, among them his beautiful queen Nafertari, for whom Ramesses II had a similar but smaller temple built near his own. The façade is further adorned at the top by decorative friezes, the uppermost consisting of a row of monkeys. The temple faced east, so that on the king's birthday or anniversary the first rays of the rising sun would light up the features of the godlike statue of Ramesses, carved in the rock on the far wall of the sanctuary together with those of the gods Ptah, Amun, and Ra-Harakhty.

An element that should be taken into account when viewing the art of that time was the relationship to their material of the vast number of sculptors and painters busy on the royal tombs in the Valley of the Kings and the monumental temples built along the valley of the Nile. Plaster mud was used to smooth the rough walls of rock-hewn tombs, but on the vast surfaces of the long halls and corridors of the huge tombs, the work was not always very neat, for the basic material for architecture was sandstone, which is rather friable and so ill adapted to the neat and precise elaboration of details.

Battle scenes were much in vogue at that period. The walls of the Ramesseum, of the temples of Karnak, Abydos, and Abu Simbel are covered with them. In a sense the subject imposed a certain simplification of form. The battle fought by Ramesses II's forces at Kadesh, immortalized in a famous poem, was one of the favourite subjects of the time. One of the clearest representations of this warlike period has been given new life by the process of restoration lavished in recent years on the reliefs of the temple at Abu Simbel. It shows the conventionally larger figure of the pharaoh on his war chariot; his horses, with great plumes on their heads, trample his enemies as they gallop on. There is a similar composition scheme in hunting scenes, which are a characteristic feature of the temple of Ramesses III at Medinet Habu (p. 163). There is undoubtedly a certain formal decadence, but the bulls' convulsions as they lie dying from the king's arrows are rendered with stark realism.

What was asked of the artist was still the same thing: to celebrate and glorify the king's deeds. Art had indeed kept its age-old social function—and it is in this light that the undoubted decline in quality due to the new mass-production character of the projects should be examined. To this must be added the fact that artists now worked on huge surfaces, and it was therefore necessary to avoid being distracted from the overall impression to be made. Artists had not lost their taste and sense of form, even if the vast size of the spaces they had to decorate did preclude a careful use of details. In any case there was no call for such use of detail as could be found in the Old Kingdom mastaba reliefs or in the tombs of important personages of the Eighteenth Dynasty. In fact the search for the utmost decorative effect led instead to a skillful use of chiaroscuro—which is why the reliefs are deeply engraved in the walls.

Finally, there was also something new in the relationship between artists and nature. The whole of Egyptian art is pervaded with a deep feeling for the natural world. It is clear even from the bas-reliefs of the Old Kingdom that the Egyptians loved trees, flowers, and vegetation. The thick clumps of papyrus and the fishing scenes were full of animals, birds, fish. Now that there was greater freedom in the choice of subject matter for tomb decoration—especially the tombs of private citizens—artists created real masterpieces: a banquet in a garden, with greenery and flowers, or a cat hunting through bushes.

There is evidence of the ancient Egyptians' love of nature even in architecture and in the decoration of temples. Of all ancient Mediterranean architectures probably none was so strongly influenced by the world around them, which was even included in the principles of the canon devised for the building of classical Egyptian temples. In the hypostyle temples, columns with palm- or lotus-shaped capitals were reminiscent of the palm trees and water plants of the Nile. Decorations with stylized plants in the lower parts of temples, and the ceilings painted blue with gold stars, are other illustrations of the close link that bound the Egyptians to nature.

A glance at the other arts of the Middle East will confirm that nowhere else did nature and landscape play such an important role as in Egypt. In no other civilization of antiquity do we find, for instance, a "botanic garden" like that on the reliefs of the temple of Thutmose III at Karnak. Clearly the Egyptians were unequalled in their time in the depiction of the natural world.

The twilight of Egyptian art—an art which had taken two thousand years to reach its apogee in the Old Kingdom—lasted another thousand years. It started towards the end of the Ramessid Dynasty, at a period known in the history of Egyptian civilization as the Low Epoch, or, in reference to the dynasties (from the Twenty-first to the Twenty-sixth), the Third Intermediate Period.

The country's dismemberment coincided with

the rule of the Twenty-first Dynasty. An autonomous state was set up in Nubia, in the southern part of the country. The pharaoh's power and authority in Egypt declined and as a result the functions and executive power of the Egyptian viceroy in Nubia were impaired. A new center of power in the region of Napata, west of the Fourth Cataract, was established, which controlled a vast territory extending down to south of the First Cataract, an area formerly under the jurisdiction of the viceroy of Nubia. The Cushite king Piankhi (751–716 B.C.), swooping up from his seat at Napata, invaded and conquered Egypt, founding there a Nubian or Ethiopian dynasty, the Twenty-fifth Dynasty. The official residence of the Nubian kings was Thebes or Tanis, but their tombs were built in the region of Napata, near the Gebel Barkal. They are in the shape of smallish and rather slender pyramids. The statue of Mentuemhet (p. 166), one of the prefects of Thebes during the Twenty-fifth Dynasty, is a characteristic Nubian portrait.

The rule of the Nubian kings may be divided into two periods. The first, called the Napatean period, lasted until 295 B.C. Then, upon the destruction of Napata, the capital was transferred to Meroe, between the Fifth and Sixth Cataracts. This second period, the Meroitic, lasted until the middle of the fourth century A.D. Its art is still Egyptian art to a great extent both in form and in content, though it is no longer a rigid imitation of New Kingdom or Saitic-period models. This can be seen in the reliefs of the great temples of Naqa and Musawarat, or, for another example, in the statue of the king of Meroe in the second century A.D.

Many indigenous decorative motifs were introduced at that time, above all in the kings' dress and the effigies of local deities unknown to the Egyptians. Classical Greco-Roman elements were also adopted. Despite the relative political isolation of the kingdom of Meroe, which lasted more than six hundred years, there were commercial contacts and wars with Egypt.

The Twenty-sixth Dynasty was founded in the city of Sais, in the Delta, by Prince Psamtik. It lasted less than a hundred years, from the seventh century B.C. to the end of the third quarter of the sixth century. Its artistic style, known as the Saitic style, exercised an important influence on the later development of Egyptian art.

The Saitic style may be defined as neoclassical, for its classicism looked back not only to the remote Old Kingdom works but also, and mostly, to models from the Eighteenth Dynasty.

Just as in New Kingdom classicism, there was in Saitic art a predilection for neatness and polished details. Its figures, which are sometimes very graceful, no longer have the balanced proportions of Eighteenth Dynasty models. Some of them, however, reveal a remote Greek influence in the softer treatment of cheeks and chin.

This neoclassical tendency of the Saitic period reappeared in the last truly Egyptian dynasty, the Thirtieth. To it we owe the masterpieces of the Road of the Sphinxes at Luxor, the portal at Karnak, and the *Mammisi*, the "Birth Sanctuary," at Dendera, built by Pharaoh Nektanebo I.

Even in periods of confusion and economic difficulties, during which artists and workshops could not work in the best possible conditions, the canon and its rigorous rules formulated more than two thousand years before still prevailed and helped to maintain a high artistic level.

The epithet "Ptolemaic" applied to a certain period in Egyptian history and art sometimes makes one forget that before Ptolemy I Soter became pharaoh in 304 B.C., Alexander the Great reigned over Egypt for nine years and after him

Philip Arrhidaeus for seven years, and finally Alexander the Great's son, Alexander IV of Macedon, for another twelve years. In Egypt the Ptolemies pursued a policy consisting of two parallel—and, in a sense, contradictory—aims: the Hellenization of the country on the one hand and the preservation of the indigenous customs on the other. Obviously this could not lead to a total compromise, a symbiosis between Egyptian and Hellenistic cultures. Nevertheless, just before Ptolemy I Soter became king of Egypt there existed all the necessary historical conditions for the possible emergence of a new Greco-Egyptian form of culture. Let us take as an illustration the famous tomb of Petosiris at Tuna el Gebel, which can be dated to the end of the fourth century B.C., about thirty years after the conquest of Egypt by Alexander the Great. In the bas-reliefs the forcefulness of Greek style stands out next to typically Egyptian scenes. There are Greek costumes and, even more important, a change in attitudes and figures which is quite new in relation to traditional Egyptian composition. The grape-harvest scene, the pressing of the grapes, and the scene of craftsmen at work are particularly fine. It is an almost complete break with the traditional and monotonous Egyptian subject matter formerly used in tombs. It may be surmised that had these seeds found a propitious ground in the land of the Nile, a completely new form of art might have emerged.

But this did not and could not take place. The Ptolemies did not look upon themselves as the founders and builders of a new Egypt, but rather as the heirs to the pharaohs. Greek culture must flourish next to Egyptian culture but the two must not become mingled. And so there existed side by side two different forms of art: the Greco-Hellenistic "Alexandrian" art and the traditionally Egyptian "Ptolemaic" art.

It is obvious that the reciprocal effect of these two artistic worlds was of great importance for the final phase in the history of Egyptian art. But in fact only a small number of monuments of the late Ptolemaic period and others of the Roman period show evidence of a certain merging of the two different arts. A very long process was necessary before this "syncretism" was reached and gave birth to a figurative art which was a compromise between Egyptian and Greek tradition.

At first glance the Ptolemaic bas-reliefs adorning the temples built at that time do not differ much in composition from the official reliefs of pharaonic art. Upon a closer look, however, the differences emerge. Bodies are softly shaped and their structure, bones, and muscles can be imagined beneath the outer envelope. In the past no Egyptian artist had ever treated the human figure in this manner; it is a feature of Greek art. Like those of the Ramessid period, Ptolemaic reliefs have a powerful sense of chiaroscuro because they are deeply carved into the surface; this also emphasizes the softness of the modelling. Even if he cannot decipher hieroglyphic writing and therefore cannot read the king's name on the reliefs, a viewer can easily distinguish works of that period from works of ancient tradition. This is the most obvious result of the coexistence of two such different cultural systems on the banks of the Nile.

In statuary, in the monuments of gods and kings of the Ptolemaic period, the rigid hieratic position is maintained. Traditional modelling is kept and even the skin is made to look dry and rigid. Only in the draperies and bodies of female statues, with their light, transparent clothes, can the influence of Greek art be felt. A new type of face appears in portraits of kings.

Even Octavian (p. 181), in his portrait in the

Page 30: Pharaoh Amenhotpe I
(1557–1530 B.C.*), XVIIIth Dynasty.*
Turin, Museo Egizio.
This statue used to be carried
about in processions on various
occasions in the Egyptian calendar
of feasts.

temple of Karnak, is shown dressed and standing in the hieratic position of the pharaoh. Other Caesars—Hadrian, for instance—were later to imitate him. It is obvious that for the Romans, the Egypt they had colonized was not a primitive African country but a country with a very ancient civilization. On the other hand the art that resulted from that encounter is insignificant. The Fayum oasis has yielded monuments that are characteristic of the Roman period in Egypt—the dark granite sculptures found at Dime, which are portraits of priests and local dignitaries of the end of the first and the beginning of the second century A.D. Similar statues have been found in Alexandria. Sometimes they are dressed in Roman clothes, which the Egyptian sculptors were unable to do well; the head is usually halfway between the Egyptian and the Greco-Roman model (a short Roman hair cut, for instance); and the polished surface of the hard stone is typically Egyptian (see the priest Hor, on the right).

The result of the Roman influence on sculpture was the creation of dry, rigid works that do not fit comfortably into either the Greco-Roman or the Egyptian tradition. It is probable, also, that the level of workmanship of sculptors' workshops was declining at that time. Artists were faced with a type of representation for which they lacked models and concrete examples, and for which the traditional canon could not be of much utility. Nor were they able at that time to elaborate a new style.

The time for that might have been a few hundred years before, at the time of the Macedonian conquest and when the tomb of Petosiris was built.

The priest Hor, *Roman period (1st century* A.D.*).*
From Alexandria. Cairo, Egyptian Museum.

29

MATERIAL AND COLOUR

A stone pyramid was built for me among
the other pyramids. The stonecutter in chief
took possession of the ground that had been
reserved, the designer in chief designed,
the sculptor in chief carved away. My
statue was covered with fine gold leaf:
His Majesty ordered it to be made.

—From *Sinuhe's Tale*, Twelfth Dynasty.

The colour illustrations reproduced from page 33 to page 64 have a purely introductory function. They offer a glimpse into the world of sculpture which is not only a three-dimensional world but also a world of colour; for sculptures are made of differently coloured materials and placed in a natural or artificial context which adds more colour. Brief captions for these are given below. The black-and-white illustrations and diagrams reproduced from page 80 to page 174 serve a more didactic function. There the reader will find, in chronological sequence, the full captions needed for an understanding of both colour and black-and-white illustrations. The page number in parentheses at the end of each caption below refers the reader to the appropriate full caption.

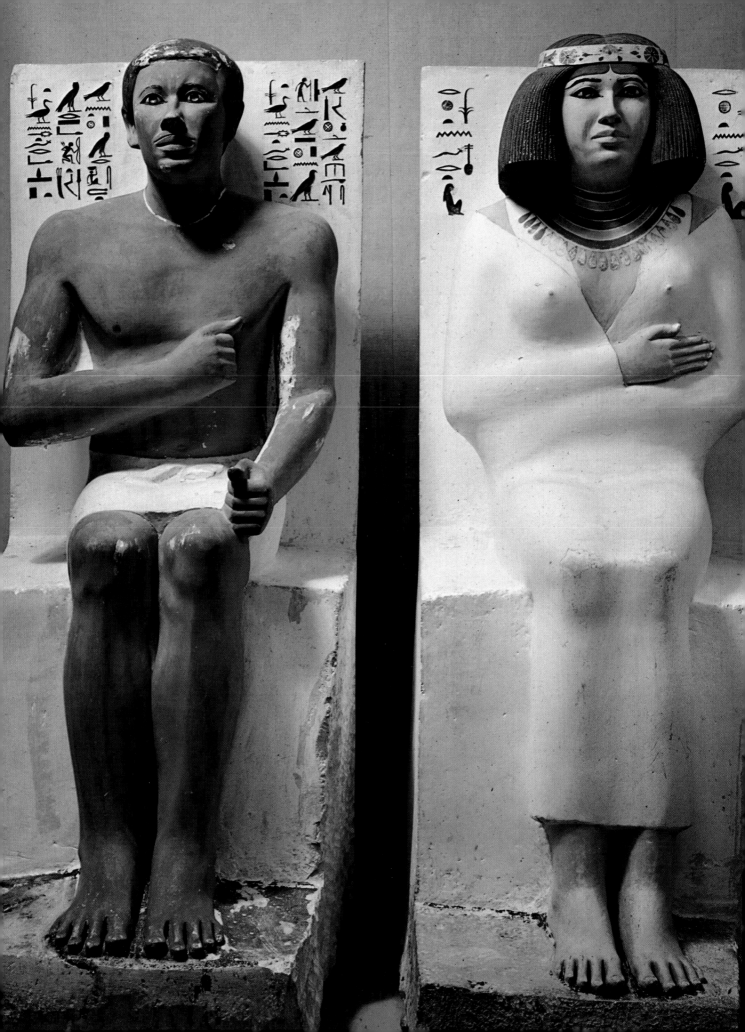

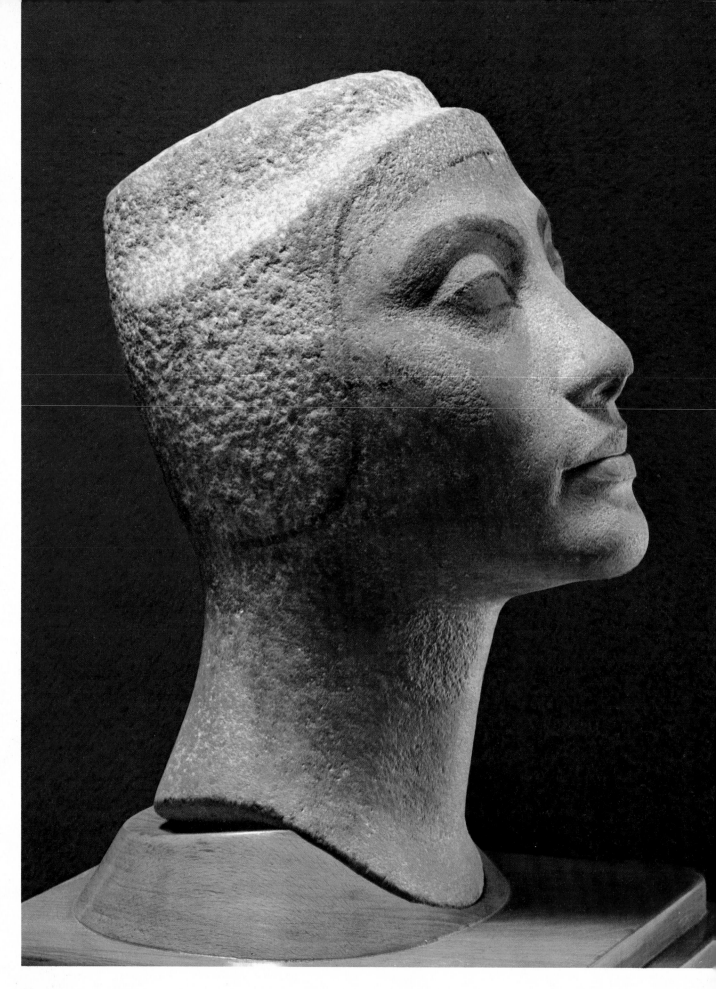

Every art, within a given society, achieves its products according to concepts and rules which are the result of instinct and experience on the part of the artist and demand on the part of those for whom they are working. The sculptor at work constitutes the secret and determining moment of a public act, a personal contribution to one's social and historical patrimony.

Working on an Egyptian statue: the finishing and polishing.

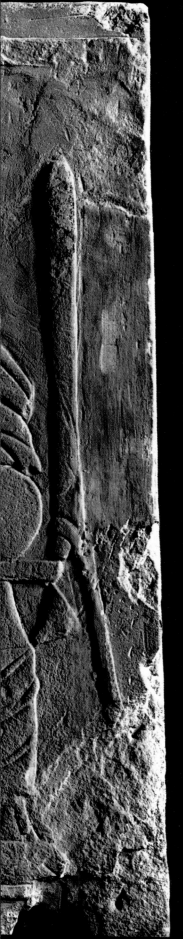

THE SCULPTOR IN PHARAONIC SOCIETY

I saw a bronze sculptor at work before his furnace. His fingers were like a crocodile's and he stank worse than leftover fish.

—From the *Satire of Trades,* Sallier Papyrus II, 4, 6.

Page 66 : Offerings to a dead woman,
XVIIIth Dynasty (1580–1314 B.C.*).*
Florence, Museo Archeologico.

Whether sculptor, painter, or goldsmith, the Egyptian artist remains anonymous, quite unlike his Greek counterpart or our modern artists whose individual personalities are so easily identified. In ancient Egypt artists never signed their works with a name or monogram, and indeed very few "signatures" of any sort have come down to us from the three thousand years of Egyptian art. In Greece the sculptor would inscribe his name—or have it inscribed by underlings—on the base of the statues he had made, and the painter would sign his paintings. Even the potter would sign his wares and the vase painter would append his name to the vases he decorated. An artist's signature also had a commercial as well as artistic significance, for it identified the workshop it came from.

The situation was quite different in Egypt. Only the king could take credit for a finished work and have a relevant inscription added to it. It was therefore the king's name and not the artist's that was transmitted to posterity. The inscriptions found on temples and monuments tell us that such-and-such a pharaoh has built such a work out of granite, limestone, or sandstone, or adorned it with precious metals in honour of his father, the God. Among thousands of works of art there is one exception: the statue of Zoser, a king of the Third Dynasty, on which the name and titles of Imhotep—the architect of the famous step pyramid at Saqqara—appear on the inscription next to the king's. It is worth noting also that this is the only inscription of the time that mentions Imhotep's name. This architect and philosopher who was later deified and worshipped until the waning of antiquity did not leave any writings. And it would be wrong to imagine that the inscription of his name on the statue of King Zoser was Imhotep's signature. It would have been unthinkable that a man of such high standing, the architect of the great

burial compound surrounding the step pyramid, could have carved that statue himself. The inscription should be taken rather as evidence of the king's recognition of his merits. There is also the possibility that Imhotep was a relative of the king's, for high officials were often chosen from among members of the royal family.

The sculptor's social position is outlined in a scene depicted in the tomb of Puimre, an aristocratic priest and architect of the time of Thutmose III (Eighteenth Dynasty). The scene represents a sculptor's workshop in which three master craftsmen and three directors of the temple workshops are giving an account to Puimre himself of the works ordered and finished—two obelisks, many objects of worship, and other similar works. The most curious aspect of the scene is that Puimre is looking at these objects of the highest artistic value and superb workmanship as if they were a load of bricks. The inscription describing the scene does not include the names of the artists standing before Puimre, nor is there a single word of thanks to them.

Other inscriptions in tombs referring to more modest commissions (those neither from the state nor from the priests) reveal that craftsmen or sculptors were employed in the decoration of tombs against a payment in kind—bread, beer, cloth, and so on. There is a very interesting inscription on the stela of Ramesses II, at Heliopolis, which describes the king's visit to the quarries of Kom el Ahmar and to the sculptors' and stonecutters' workshops there. The text mentions that these craftsmen were given enough food to last them for the duration of their work, but the portions allotted them were obviously insufficient and in some cases just enough to prevent them from dying of hunger; in any case they had to last until the work commissioned by the king was finished. There is more evidence of cases like this one, especially towards the end of the New

Kingdom. There are documents of the Twentieth Dynasty revealing that the craftsmen working on the necropolis of the Valley of the Kings were compelled to organize a strike to obtain the payment they were owed. The hungry workmen arrived in procession before the king's palace and were finally placated by court officials who had been sent to parley with them. It was a time of economic hardship and they were not paid in full at once but were given a part payment with the promise that they would soon be paid in full.

It should be noted, however, that standards of living varied greatly within the social category to which sculptors or craftsmen belonged. Some of them could afford splendidly decorated tombs and the inscriptions in them reveal that the standard of living was rather high.

Even if on the whole ancient Egyptian artists remained anonymous, nevertheless a certain number of names—and even biographies—have trickled down to us, mostly through inscriptions. There were not many. As far as sculptors are concerned, we know eleven names from the Old Kingdom period and fifteen from the New Kingdom. We have, however, a greater number of names of painters and architects.

The "signatures" that have come down to us can be divided into two categories: "portraits" and "marginals." The craftsman who was commissioned to decorate the interior of a tomb, for instance, could sometimes sneak in his name or even his portrait, in the hope that at least this part of his personality would live on for eternity in a safe place. There are some curious examples. One painter, for example, wrote in the tomb he was decorating that he was not "just any painter who could be ordered about, but rather an able-fingered writer from the temple of Khnum [at Esna], whom the high priest [at El Kab] sent for himself, and who

supervised the work with all his heart." Scribes, in fact, often scorned the work of artists. It was a scribe who, in the Sallier Papyrus (in what is known as the *Satire of Trades*), says he never knew of a sculptor or goldsmith who was ever given a state commission. "But rather," he says, "I saw a bronze sculptor at work before his furnace. His fingers were like a crocodile's and he stank worse than leftover fish."

Artists and craftsmen were under the protection of the god of Memphis, Ptah; so it was Ptah's high priest who was in charge of them. Because of this his titles were "Great Master of Art" or "Chief of Artists." This did not mean that some of the most gifted artists or craftsmen did not rise to the position of "Chief Craftsman" or "Chief" Sculptor, Painter, or Goldsmith. As for professional organizations, there were artists' fraternities similar to the medieval guilds.

Some light on the collective character of artists' work is shed by the list of specialized artists who made up the teams working in a sculptor's workshop: there was, for instance, an artist who specialized in drawing outlines; another who dealt with plasterwork; another whose job was to prepare the plaster; a stonecutter; a relief specialist; one who cut statues into shape; another who modelled them; yet another whose job was to smooth them and polish them; there was an artist whose task was solely to paint statues; another who painted temple walls; and so on. Apart from the artists themselves, these teams also included auxiliary workers. The payrolls that scribes carefully prepared for the patrons include, after the artists' names, those of porters, building site attendants, and in later times even slaves whose task was to bring the others water from the Nile and perform other menial tasks for them. It is interesting that occasionally these payrolls include a doctor whose job it was to look after the workers' health.

Unfortunately we know very little of the qualifications of such doctors. Excavations by a French archeological team at Deir el Medineh have brought to light valuable documents concerning the daily life of the artists and craftsmen who worked on the decoration of the royal tombs in the Valley of the Kings at the end of the second millennium B.C.

These documents reveal not only the daily life of the workers but also the difficulties they encountered in their work. Certain texts even mentioned thefts committed by a group of workmen. It may be that at the time (the Twentieth Dynasty) there was no longer proper control of the workers and that chaos reigned in artists' organizations. Nevertheless the craftsman's or stonecutter's condition until the end of the New Kingdom was that of a free man. Each worker received a specific sum for his contribution, and it was only later that slaves were used in this capacity.

The famous American archeologist George Reisner, while he was excavating the neighbourhood of the funerary temple of Pharaoh Mycerinus at Giza, discovered thirty-eight statues of a king, carved in hard stone and left unfinished in different stages of production. The statues bore the marks of the tools that had been used in each of these stages, and upon a careful analysis of this fascinating material Reisner managed to distinguish eight basic stages in the production of statues. According to him the first four stages were the work of assistants, whereas the last four were done by the master sculptor himself. Reisner's observations are extremely interesting and probably correct; but in the light of A. H. Gardiner's research on onomatology there remains some doubt about whether the individual phases of the work can be divided among assistants and master sculptor. Above all, as has been said before, the Egyptian artist's individual talent is hard to identify in the modern or even the Greek sense, since the sculpture of ancient Egypt was based on teamwork undertaken by specialized workshops in which the chief artists were in a way similar to present-day sculptors who are the heads of ateliers.

This kind of organization, which precluded the development of a strong tendency towards individuality, was possible only in the context of the canon that determined the rules concerning representation of the human figure both in statuary and in relief work. The habit of distributing models and examples—such an example was provided, according to some scholars, by the famous head of Nafertiti found at Tell el ʿAmarna and now in the Berlin Museum—to provincial workshops meant that models of any size could be made almost automatically. It is obvious that the quality of a work of art depended to a large extent on the personality and competence of the head of the workshop, who would supervise every phase of the work from the block of stone to the finished product.

The basic tools used for stonework were stone hammers, chisels, and copper or flint augers. Quartzite or granite could be sculpted only with stone tools and soft stone only with copper tools. In preparatory stages a wide-bladed copper saw was used, together with a dampened abrasive powder. This enabled the craftsmen to gradually slice flat strips of stone from the main block in such a way that the basic shape of the statue would slowly emerge. Hammers or mallets were used, as well as stones of different shapes and degrees of hardness which served to smooth the surface of the statue. In the finishing stages small chisels were used, and to gouge out small holes such as nostrils the craftsmen used augers sometimes only a few millimeters wide. All these tools were consistently used by sculptors and stonecutters from the earliest days of Egyptian sculpture—that is, in the predynastic period—to

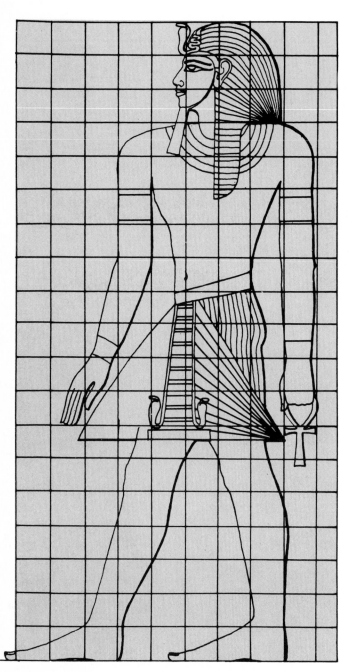

Diagram showing the division of the human figure according to the Egyptian canon.

the New Kingdom period, when bronze tools began to replace copper tools. Even after that the shapes and types of tools remained the same, until iron instruments were introduced much later. The New Kingdom saw another innovation in the production of works of art: a process that consisted of the separate modelling of various parts of a statue which were then put together. Nevertheless, the insignificance of the changes that occurred in the technique of sculpture during the entire extent of the history of Egyptian art can be seen from the comparison between unfinished statues of Akhenaton's time and similar objects of Mycerinus's time.

The principle of depicting the human figure on a flat surface according to its maximum dimensions in breadth, a principle shared by all "primitive" arts, was present in Egypt from prehistoric and predynastic times. According to this principle the trunk was more or less in the shape of a triangle and the arms, legs, and head were depicted in profile.

This traditional outline which people were used to for thousands of years did not stop artists from searching for a higher degree of realism in their figurative scheme. There was a need, therefore, to develop and fix relative proportions of the human figure which corresponded to reality and could at the same time be made into norms. It took a long time, and many experiments, before the definitive result was reached—and that was a real discovery. In the famous tablet of Narmer, described in detail in the first chapter (pp. 10–11), the heads are still too large in relation to the height of the figures. Later the human figure was determined by strict proportional relations.

The human figure in a standing position was drawn on a sheet of papyrus or a stone slab in such a way as to be contained within a length of eighteen squares (see p. 72). The hair above the forehead was contained within an extra row of squares. For the rest the proportions were as follows: from the hair below the forehead to the base of the neck, two rows of squares; from the neck to the knee, another ten rows; and from the knee to the base of the feet, six rows. The human figure in a sitting position rated fourteen rows of squares, or fifteen if you counted the hair. This scheme prevailed until the end of the history of Egyptian art, although from the Twenty-sixth Dynasty (the Saitic) onwards the number of rows of squares rose to twenty-one and a quarter.

These models drawn on papyrus were used for painting and relief work, for the representation of the human figure on a flat surface. In statuary, however, stone or plaster models were used as guidelines. But even here the subdivision into squares could be useful and indeed some of the smaller models had a system of squares inscribed on their flatter parts, such as the headdress, or on their lower parts, or else on the back. Points were used to determine the proportions of larger works based on the small models.

An enlightening anecdote was related by Diodorus, a Greek historian living in the first century B.C. He tells us that two sculptors, Telecles and Theodorus of Samos, decided one day to collaborate on a statue of the Pythian Apollo, basing their work on the Egyptian modular scheme of the time, which divided the standing human figure into twenty-one and a quarter equal parts. Each of the two artists worked separately on one half of the statue, and when they put the two halves together they discovered that they fitted perfectly.

What seemed an extraordinary feat to Diodorus was certainly taken quite for granted by the Egyptians, for the rules of the canon were extremely strict and left no room for doubt as far as the placing of the tiniest detail of a human figure was concerned.

As we have said, on a flat surface the human figure had to be depicted in profile. This principle, however, was applied in a peculiar way: within the head, drawn in profile, the eye is drawn frontally; so are the shoulders. Both arms had to be seen, and both hands with all the fingers. It is obvious that this way of twisting one's neck is impossible and therefore totally unrealistic. In the rest of the figure, too, the stipulated regulations are a distortion of reality. The thorax is depicted frontally, but at about the level of the abdomen the body is suddenly twisted into a profile position, which results in the navel's being drawn on the external margin of the silhouette. In the female figure the breasts are drawn in profile immediately below the frontally drawn shoulders. The legs are in profile and the feet are usually seen from the inside.

In choosing the way the figure faced, the artist, if he was free to do so, would always prefer the right profile; in other words, the profile of a figure which faces towards the right. The canon stipulated one of two positions for the human figure: a walking or a sitting position. Gestures were of course conditioned by this: if an arm had to be extended, it would be the left arm, while the right would be shown hanging down.

Dress and ornaments changed according to the historical period, but they were always a binding element in the representation of a figure. Only children were ever represented in the nude. During the Old Kingdom the standard male attire of the Egyptians was a kind of short skirt or apron, which later became much longer. Necklaces and breast-plates changed according to the historical context, but the original modular scheme of squares included some details of dress, such as the apron pleated over the hips which was characteristic of the Old Kingdom.

The first models based on the scheme of squares were probably made in the workshops of Memphis, which was at that time the capital of Egypt. From Memphis they were sent to the main provincial centers where temples and the tombs of high officials needed to be decorated. These models left no room for error and it was easy to transpose into the final dimensions the drawings on papyrus or the model engraved onto a slab of stone. If a provincial artist received, for instance, the model of a male or female figure facing right, and by chance had to decorate both sides of a portal, he would reverse the figure, using his initiative as best he could. In such cases there might be some difficulty in positioning the arms, say, or else—and this could be even worse—in finding the exact spot for the pleats of the dress. On the whole, however, this system of models was efficient, and it was one of the elements that helped to maintain a high level of workmanship for many centuries.

This did not mean, however, that the sculptors of ancient Egypt were never capable of slovenly work. The Polish excavations of the temple of Thutmose III at Deir el Bahri brought to light the fact that the side of one of the wall blocks that were so magnificently sculpted and coloured was uneven and looked as if it were crumbling. In fact, it looked, at first glance, as if the block had been damaged by falling while it was being worked on. But this was not true. A sign painted in red was discovered on the surface of the damaged stone, under the coat of plaster that covered it. The blocks bearing reliefs had all been individually marked with these red signs during the construction of the temple for recognition and control purposes. And so the existence of this sign on the block with the crumbling surface meant that it had been checked when completed and that those in charge of the construction of the temple had been in a hurry and had preferred to use imperfect blocks, covering the defective parts with plaster. Indeed, the use of plaster to cover up a rough stone surface was quite common in tombs hewn out of the rock and had been so since the Fourth Dynasty. When the rock consisted of porous stone which could not be made perfectly smooth, a coat of plaster was applied before the artists could get on with the decoration— bas-reliefs or hieroglyphics—of the walls. Many examples of this can be found in the royal tombs of the New Kingdom. Plaster was also used, of course, to hide any defects that might appear during work on the bas-reliefs, and these retouchings were revealed only if the piece of plaster fell away; otherwise they would never be noticed.

It is worth mentioning at this point a detail that was the object of much speculation until not so long ago. It concerns the nature of the light available to the sculptors while they were at work on the reliefs (which were later coloured) in the tombs deeply hewn out of the rock in the Valley of the Kings. They could not have used torches or oil lamps, for these would have smoked and blackened the walls, thereby making the work impossible; and no trace of soot has been found in any of these tombs. It has been suggested that the workers may have used some kind of reflecting screen which, like a mirror, reflected the sunlight that fell into the tomb. Experiments trying to recreate these conditions failed, however, for it was discovered that in the subterranean tombs there could not have been a single ray of sunlight. It was only in recent years that this apparently insoluble mystery was satisfactorily solved by one of the greatest Egyptologists, Jaroslav Cerny. Examining the texts concerning the list of materials delivered to the artists working on rock tombs, Cerny discovered that candles made of fat mixed with natron (and in all probability made in the Wadi el Natrun) were used as lamps, because they did not produce blackening smoke.

The Egyptian artists used several types of relief.

These included the conventional relief, "flat" relief; then the gouged-out relief, the so-called *relief en creux*; and the "inlaid" relief, which was not often used and first appeared in the Fourth Dynasty, in tombs at Meidum and Abu Roash, on the edge of the Memphis necropolis. Finally there was the so-called high relief, a convex-looking relief which has nothing to do with statuary. In all these reliefs the slight differences and subtleties which distinguished the work of one workshop from another can be discerned only by the trained eye of a specialist.

There were certainly differences too in the representation of the human figure, walking or seated, in the Old Kingdom, the New Kingdom, and even more in the Ptolemaic period. We examined some of these differences earlier, but they were unimportant ones that never affected the basic stylistic form, that form which, by virtue of the canon regulating the representation of the human figure, gave Egyptian art its homogeneity, individuality, and exceptional quality for three thousand years.

Each artistic discovery that becomes crystallized into a norm begins after a while to have negative results next to its more positive ones. To our minds today, the rules and restrictions imposed on ancient Egyptian artists may seem such as to cramp an artist's creativity. But this was not so. Egyptian society was well used to rigid conditions in social hierarchy, and even the rhythm of life was regulated by the flooding of the Nile which determined the sequence of work. Thus the Egyptian could appreciate an art which was as consistent and restricted as his own life and experience: the season of the Nile's flood returned every year, the sun always burned fiercely, the stars always kept the same patterns, the air was always filled with the noise of the winches and pulleys that drew water from the canals. And yet even within the rigid system of rules and regulations of the canon there was always some room for inventiveness. There were some artists who modified the arrangement in horizontal strips of bas-reliefs; others who changed the pattern of the narrative; others still who dared to represent parts of the human figure from the back (this, however, happened only in the New Kingdom). And finally there were the differences caused by unevenness of workmanship, for next to many magnificent works works of much poorer quality can also be found.

What we have said so far, however, does not explain how the canon came about. To understand this we need to examine the conditions of work in artists' workshops, the way they were organized, and the function and position of the artist.

The essence of the canon is not restricted to the representation of the human figure alone. It encompasses a much vaster area which goes beyond the development of a technical pattern for depicting the human figure on a flat surface, the relations of various proportions, and their practical application in the transposition of figures and narratives established by models in larger reliefs or paintings.

In regard to the artist we have already seen what a high degree of specialization there was in the production of bas-reliefs and statues. The same was true for goldsmiths. Washing the metal, for instance, was done by a special category of workers; there were others who took care of the furnaces; still others who did the modelling; artists whose duty consisted in engraving the objects; and other artists who polished the finished work. There were craftsmen whose job was to cut facets on precious stones, others who inlaid them. The operation of putting together the various elements of a breastplate was also entrusted to a specialist. An artist was therefore never in a position to handle a work by himself, from the beginning to the end.

This was the general state of affairs, even outside artistic production; it is amusing to note that the maximum specialization occurred in the profession of pastry making.

Artists' workshops were near the treasury or the temples. The profession and also the know-how were passed down from father to son. There is mention of one family who for seven generations held the title of "Head of the painters of Amun." The Egyptian system, therefore, fostered the development not of individual artists but of specialists. This of course led to a division of the profession into castes. In the social context the profession of sculptor or goldsmith was considered inferior to that of scribe. In reality the artist was indeed a mere craftsman, just like the carpenter, the baker, the weaver, the tailor, or the washerman, who were all part of the third social group, that of the men who worked with their hands. This group, however, was superior in the social scale to farmers, fishermen, and shepherds.

The fact that he was considered a craftsman did not put the Egyptian artist in a different position from, let us say, his Greek counterpart. It should be remembered that characters such as the sculptor Phidias, or the painters Zeuxis and Apelles, who reached a very high position in the society of their time, were exceptional cases. In Greece too, sculptors and painters were considered craftsmen— *banausoi*—men who worked with their hands.

The architect, on the other hand, had a completely different social position. He belonged to a higher social category, that of the functionaries, and was shown much more respect than sculptors or painters. As the sole repository of the secrets of his profession, he was even more important than the scribe. It was not the fact that they could build temples for the gods or palaces for the kings that bestowed upon architects their privileged position in the Egyptian social hierarchy. It was rather the fact that they were the only ones who could design and build royal tombs.

". . . so that no one could see or hear . . ." says an inscription outlining the aim of the architect Inenis, working on the tomb of Thutmose I. Other "directors of projects" expressed themselves in a similar vein. For the architect was the protector not only of the safety of the body from profanation, and the protector of the funerary treasures from theft, but also and above all the protector of the secret of the whereabouts of the entrance to the tomb. If the architect was the one who provided the material dwelling place for the *ka*, the king's spiritual personality, he was therefore the one on whom favourable conditions for the king's journey in his life beyond depended. Such responsibility obviously merited an adequate recognition.

A cubit of gold was found in the tomb of the architect Tcha, head of architects at the time of Amenhotpe III. This is not surprising if one thinks of the motives the king must have had to seek the favours of the man responsible for building his tomb. The work of any sculptor or painter could be substituted for that of another; but changing architects in the course of the building of a tomb meant not so much a risk of jeopardizing the solidity of the building, but rather jeopardizing the safeguarding of the secret of the tomb's entrance. In this light it is easy to understand how it was possible for architects such as Imhotep, Senmut, Amenhotpe son of Hapy, and others to rise to such exalted positions. This did not mean that these artists, who were given such honours during their lifetime and also after death, never experienced downfall. Senmut was of humble origin, but the quality of his work was such that he was eventually entrusted with the most important state commissions during the reign of Queen Hatshepsut. It was he who built for her the magnificent temple at Deir el Bahri and those at Karnak and Hermonthis. Apart from his functions as court architect, he also fulfilled those of chancellor of state and tutor to the queen's daughter. It has not been proved conclusively that he was the queen's lover after she was widowed. It was during his protectress's lifetime that Senmut's downfall occurred. For having reached such an exalted position had gone to his head and he apparently lost all sense of reality. He went so far as to build his own tomb within the sacred precinct of Hatshepsut's temple at Deir el Bahri, carefully masking its entrance. He also put his own portraits in various chapels of the temple he had built for the queen.

The portraits were carefully placed, so that when the double doors of the chapel were opened the priests could not see them. Nevertheless, when the chapel doors were closed the portraits of Senmut remained face to face with the statues of the gods. Considering the religious ideology of the time, the action was nothing less than sacrilegious. When the portraits were discovered Senmut was deposed from office and never again appeared in public. After that he could not expect that when he died his mummy would be placed in the tomb he had had built for himself within Hatshepsut's compound, so he built himself another tomb in the necropolis reserved for ordinary mortals. His portraits were of course removed from the chapels, except for one which was overlooked. Senmut placed it in a niche in the rock-hewn sanctuary of the goddess Hathor.

The situation of architects in Greek and Roman antiquity was altogether different, and no architect ever rose to such heights as Senmut. Even Ictinus, who built the Parthenon, took his orders from Phidias, and as for the Roman architects, their role was always that of a subordinate. It was only at the very end of antiquity that the situation of architects became somewhat similar to that of Inenis, Hapusoneb, Puimre, Hori, Suti, and many others besides Imhotep, Amenhotpe son of Hapy, and Senmut. Cassiodorus, senator and secretary of Theodoric, king of the Goths, gives the text of a decree addressed by the king to the architect in charge of public works. In it the king mentions the honours and glory attached to the office: "You must also appreciate the kindness with which you are treated: among his many followers, you, bearing the golden rod, walk before the king himself."

It is an amazing fact that during the whole course of the three-thousand-year history of ancient Egypt, certain aspects of the social hierarchy which were fixed as far back as the beginning of the Old Kingdom were maintained intact until the very end of that civilization. One might have thought that the structure of social hierarchy would have been affected at least by the social revolution which took place towards the end of the Sixth Dynasty and led to a temporary dissolution of the state. But it was quite otherwise, and after the First Intermediate Period everything went back to what it had been, and although the kings may not have felt as secure as those of the Old Kingdom, the position of artists was unchanged. The next few periods of political unrest saw the same phenomenon. The sculptors who created the magnificent statues of Chephren, the triads of Mycerinus, those who had adorned the fifth-century mastabas with splendid bas-reliefs, those who had served the Ptolemaic kings or the Roman overlords—all these artists were treated on a par with stonecutters and craftsmen. If any of them, through talent or cleverness, rose to the rank of head of his workshop or group leader, this served only to improve his own material situation and make his life more comfortable. It had no influence whatsoever on his social role in the rigorous hierarchy of ancient Egypt.

THE WORKS

**Art knows no frontiers, but no artist
will ever reach perfection.**

**—from the collection of
maxims of the minister
Ptahhotep, Fifth Dynasty.**

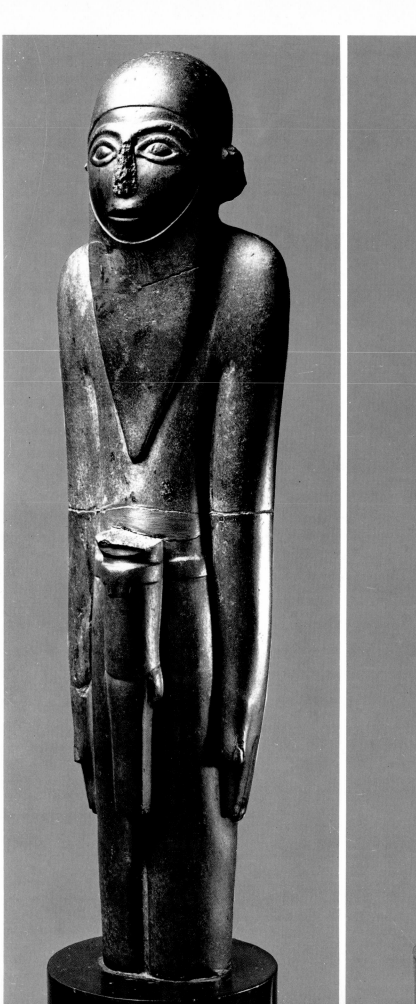

Above: Fragment of a votive tablet,
*predynastic period (*c. *3300* B.C.*). Schist; height 30 cm.
Cairo, Egyptian Museum.*
The tablet commemorates an Egyptian victory, probably over
Libyan tribes (according to the hieroglyphics in the bottom
right-hand corner), through the symbolic representation of
animals and plants. The tablet was used as a palette for
mixing antimony, the black cosmetic used in eye makeup.

Left: Figure of a man *(front and profile),*
predynastic period (IVth millennium B.C.*).*
Basalt; height 39·4 cm.
Oxford, Ashmolean Museum.
This probably represents a native of Lower Egypt or Libya,
with a long beard, loincloth, and clinging headgear.

Right: Vase in the shape of a woman, *predynastic*
*period (*c. *3500* B.C.*).*
Painted terra cotta; height 34·5 cm.
Oxford, Ashmolean Museum.
This funerary vase in the shape of a large-hipped woman is
based on a typology common to all Mediterranean
civilizations of that time, which represents the "Mother
Goddess." The vase dates from the first Naqada culture.

Left: Lion, *Ist–IInd Dynasty (*c. *3000–2778 B.C.).*
Red earthenware; height 42·4 cm.
Oxford, Ashmolean Museum.
In every Mediterranean civilization the lion symbolizes
strength (both physical and moral), and therefore royalty.
This magical object is the predecessor of the sphinx.
From Hierakonpolis.

Above: Hippopotamus, *predynastic period (*c. *3000 B.C.).*
Alabaster; height 17 cm., length 32 cm.
Copenhagen, Ny Carlsberg Glyptotek.
The magic figure of the hippopotamus represents a peace-
loving but powerful deity. Later on, in the historical period,
the hippopotamus came to represent Thueris, the goddess of
fertility and patron goddess of pregnant women.

Left: Hetepdief, IInd dynasty (29th century B.C.).
Red granite; height 39 cm.
Cairo, Egyptian Museum.
This statuette probably represents a Memphite priest who served the first three kings of the IInd Dynasty (whose names are engraved on his back). He is shown kneeling in what is almost certainly a praying attitude.
From Mitrahina.

Right: The Princess Rezi, IIIrd Dynasty (2778–2723 B.C.). *Diorite; height 83 cm. Turin, Museo Egizio. The princess is shown sitting in the attitude of resurrection, with her left hand beneath her breast and her right hand extended towards the food offerings (which will sustain her in the world beyond). The seat is in the shape of the wooden throne used at the time. Rezi is wearing a wig, a long linen robe, and numerous bracelets. Her name and titles are engraved on the socle.*

Left : Sepa and Nedji, *IIIrd Dynasty*
(2778–2723 B.C.*)*.
Painted limestone ;
height of male figure 165 cm. ;
height of female figure 159 cm.
Paris, Louvre.
This pair of statues represents two
members of the royal family. Sepa, who
held a lofty religious position, is shown
holding the symbols of power : the staff in
his left hand and the scepter in his right
hand. His wife is wearing a wig and a
long linen robe ; both wrists are adorned
with bracelets.

Right : Detail of Nesa, *profile.*

Page 33 : Pharaoh Zoser *(detail),*
IIIrd Dynasty (2778–2723 B.C.*)*.
White limestone ; height 140 cm.
Cairo, Egyptian Museum.
The pharaoh is shown seated on a high-
backed throne ; he is wearing a linen
headdress and the ceremonial false
beard. His right hand, balled into a fist
on his breast, contains an amulet ; his left
hand is extended towards the ritual
offerings which sustain the dead in their
life beyond. The statue comes from the
king's tomb, the step pyramid of
Saqqara ; it was found in the serdab, *a*
completely walled room next to the
burial chamber. Though it remained
invisible, the statue "looked out" onto
the burial chamber through two narrow
openings. According to religious belief, it
represented the pharaoh's soul.

Above: Pharaoh Radadef, *IVth Dynasty (2723–2563* B.C.*).*
Quartzite; height 28 cm.
Paris, Louvre.
The king's head, a fragment of a lost statue, is covered with a linen headdress, with the frontal representation of the sacred asp.

Left: Hesyra, *IIIrd Dynasty (2778–2723* B.C.*).*
Bas-relief; wood; height 114 cm.
Cairo, Egyptian Museum.
This relief was part of a series of eleven panels lining the niches in the tomb of Hesyra at Saqqara. A high official of Pharaoh Zoser, Hesyra is shown here with a scribe's instruments.

Right and page 34: Pharaoh Chephren,
IVth Dynasty (2723–2563 B.C.*).*
Black diorite, veined with white;
height 168 cm.
Cairo, Egyptian Museum.
Chephren, seated on a high-backed throne, is shown wearing the ceremonial beard. His head is under the protection of the falcon-headed god Horus, who is embodied by the pharaohs. The throne has lion-shaped legs—symbol of royalty—and a relief on its sides refers to the union of the kingdoms of Upper and Lower Egypt, represented by the intertwined symbols of the lotus and the papyrus.
From Chephren's temple at Giza.

Left: Pharaoh Mycerinus between
the Goddess Hathor and
the *Nomos* of Cynopolis,
IVth Dynasty (2723–2563 B.C.).
Green schist; height 95·5 cm.
Cairo, Egyptian Museum.
*The pharaoh is shown wearing the
ceremonial beard and the crown of
Upper Egypt. He is holding by the hand
the sky goddess Hathor, shown on his
right, with the solar disc held between
her horns. The pair may symbolize either
the union between the goddess and the
pharaoh in the world of the dead, or the
birth of the crown prince, according to
the belief in the direct divine descent of
the king. The female divinity on the
pharaoh's left represents the nomos
(province) of Cynopolis, in Upper
Egypt, symbolized by the "Black Dog,"
whose profile is carved above the
goddess's head. From the king's sacred
place in Giza.*

Page 35: Pharaoh Chephren,
IVth Dynasty (2723–2563 B.C.).
Translucent alabaster; height 80 cm.
Cairo, Egyptian Museum.
*This is another version, in a smaller size,
of the statue on page 89, this time with a
cube-shaped seat. The statue, which was
polychrome originally, still shows traces
of colour. It is sometimes described as a
copy of the Saitic period.*

Right: Pharaoh Sahura and the
Nomos of Koptos,
Vth Dynasty (2563–2423 B.C.).
Diorite; height 63·5 cm.
Metropolitan Museum of Art.
*This group shows the pharaoh, wearing a
linen headdress and the uraeus, with the
female patron divinity of the province of
Koptos, in Upper Egypt.*

Left: Pharaoh Userkaef *(?),*
Vth Dynasty *(2563–2423* B.C.*).*
Schist; life size.
Cairo, Egyptian Museum.
*This head, a fragment of a lost
statue, is wearing the
crown of Lower Egypt.
From Abu Sir.*

Right: Pharaoh Pepy I *(detail),*
VIth Dynasty *(2423–2263* B.C.*).*
Copper; height 177 cm.
Cairo, Egyptian Museum.
*This statue used to stand in the temple of
Hierakonpolis, next to a similar but
much smaller statue (60 cm., not
illustrated), probably representing the
king's son, the future Pepy II, or his
younger brother Merenra. These two
works are a very rare example of early
copper statuary. The technique of metal
casting was used for the heads only; the
bodies are made of strips of hammered
copper applied over a wooden structure.*

93

Right: The Prince Ankhhaf,
IVth Dynasty (2723–2563 B.C.*).*
Limestone covered in painted
stucco; height 50·6 cm.
Boston, Museum of Fine Arts.
Ankhhaf, son-in-law of Cheops and
chancellor of Chephren, is portrayed
here in a bust, a very rare form of
portraiture in Egyptian art. The bust was
found in the prince's tomb in Giza, near
the pyramid of Cheops.

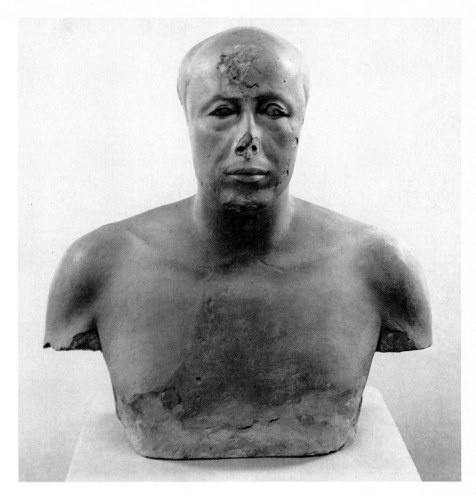

Left: A "replacement head,"
IVth Dynasty (2723–2563 B.C.*).*
Limestone; height 19·5 cm.
Cairo, Egyptian Museum.
About twenty such heads are known to
exist. They come from Giza and were
found next to the sarcophagus in IVth
Dynasty tombs which were bare of any
other statues. They may have been
connected with some unknown local
ritual.

Pages 94 and 95 (details) and
page 36 (whole): Rahotep and
Nofret,
IVth Dynasty (2723–2563 B.C.*).*
Painted limestone, with inlaid eyes
(quartz and rock crystal); height of
the male figure 120 cm.; height of the
female figure 118 cm.
Cairo, Egyptian Museum.
These two works, found in a perfect
state of preservation in a tomb at
Meidum, represent a prince of the

blood—probably the son of Pharaoh
Snefru, general and high priest of
Heliopolis—and his consort.
They are seated on cube-shaped, high-
backed seats with hieroglyphics giving
their titles.
The golden colour of Nofret's skin
corresponds to the canons of female
beauty of the period.

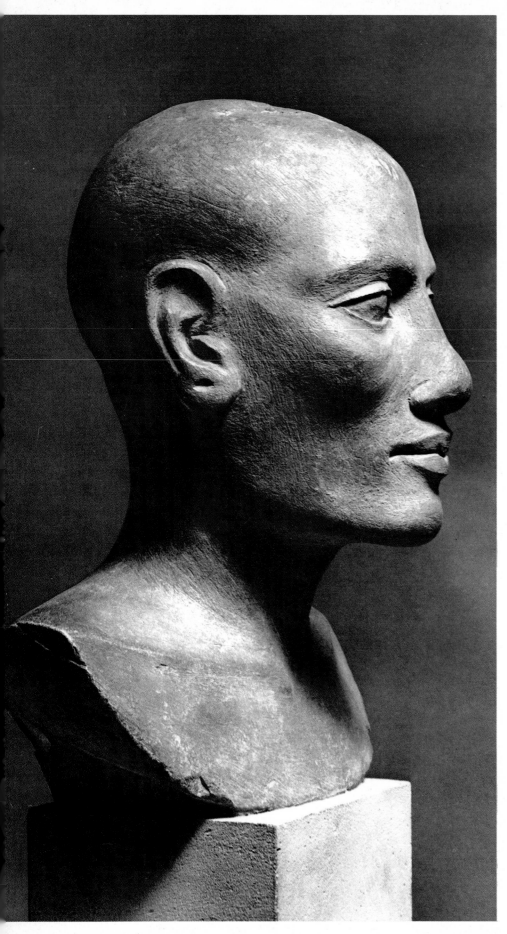

Left: Head of a man,
Vth Dynasty (2563–2423 B.C.*).*
Painted limestone; height 34 cm.
Paris, Louvre.
This portrait of unknown origin is also known as the "Salt Head," after the collection to which it formerly belonged.

Page 37: The "Sheikh el Beled,"
IVth Dynasty (2723–2563 B.C.*).*
Sycamore wood, with inlaid eyes; height 110 cm.
Cairo, Egyptian Museum.
This statue represents the high priest Ka-aper (see also page 106); the stick indicates his aristocratic rank and the scepter (now lost) which was held in the right hand denotes his position as an official. The arms were made separately and stuck onto the body according to the technique used at that time. Originally the statue was covered in polychrome stucco; the feet and the stick have been restored. The name by which the work is known traditionally is due to the exclamations of the Egyptian workmen who, when they brought it up to the light from a tomb near Saqqara, saw in it a resemblance to the head (sheikh) of their village.

Right: The Dwarf Khnumhetep,
VIth Dynasty (2423–2263 B.C.*).*
Painted limestone; height 47 cm.
Cairo, Egyptian Museum.
The character portrayed here was "Superintendent to the Wardrobe of Funerary Priests."

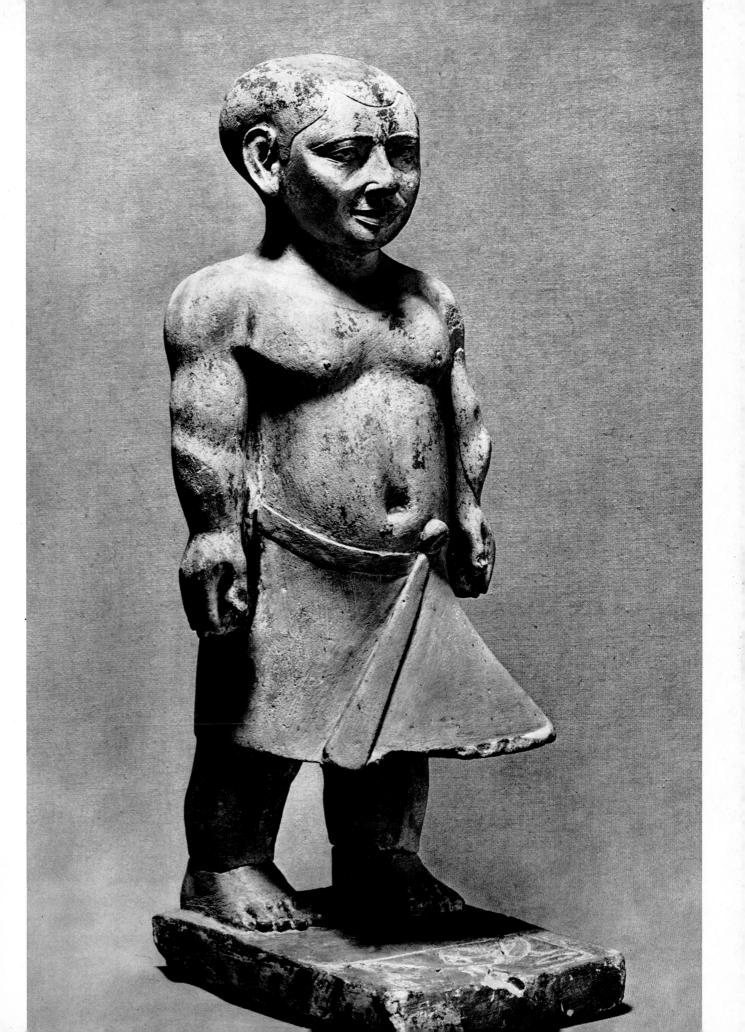

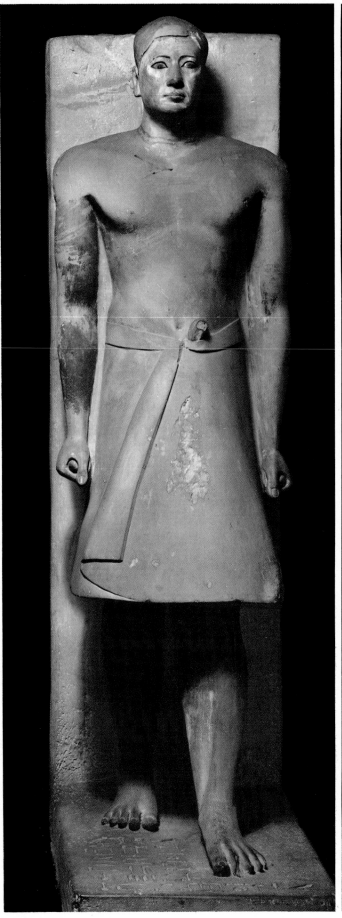

Opposite, left: Ranefer,
Vth Dynasty (2563–2423 B.C.*).*
Painted limestone; height 185 cm.
Cairo, Egyptian Museum.
*Ranefer, high priest of Ptah, god of
craftsmen, is represented bareheaded
and dressed in everyday clothes; he is
holding in his right hand the small
scepter of officials.*

Opposite, right, and this page:
Ranefer, *Vth Dynasty
(2563–2423* B.C.*), whole and detail.*
Painted limestone; height 180 cm.
Cairo, Egyptian Museum.
*The priest is shown wearing ceremonial
dress and a wig. Both statues were found
in Ranefer's burial chamber at Saqqara.*

Page 43: The Dwarf Seneb
and his family, *VIth Dynasty
(2423–2263* B.C.*).*
Painted limestone; height 33 cm.
Cairo, Egyptian Museum.
*Seneb, the superintendent of the royal
weaving manufacture, is represented
with his wife, a member of the ruling
family. Before their seat, and in smaller
scale, are the figures of their children,
completely naked according to the
Egyptian custom of clothing children
only after adolescence.*
From the Giza necropolis.

Above: A group of cranes, *Vth Dynasty (2563–2423* B.C.*).*
Limestone bas-relief; height 31 cm.
Saqqara, mastaba of Ti.
This zoomorphic relief, of a type commonly found in
Memphite tombs, is part of the wall decorations of Ti's
mastaba (a tomb built above the ground).

Left: Ti *(detail), Vth Dynasty (2563–2423* B.C.*).*
Painted limestone; height 200 cm.
Cairo, Egyptian Museum.
The official Ti was the administrator in charge of the
funerary temples under two pharaohs of the Vth Dynasty.
The statue, which represents him wearing the ceremonial
dress and the short wig, was found in the burial chamber in
his tomb at Saqqara.

Page 41: The produce of the fields,
Vth Dynasty (2563–2423 B.C.*).*
Bas-relief, painted limestone; height c. *30 cm.*
Saqqara, mastaba of Ti.
The servants with baskets of food represent the produce
yielded by the lands administered by the official Ti.

Page 40: Preparations for a banquet,
Vth Dynasty (2563–2423 B.C.*).*
Bas-relief, painted limestone; height 35 cm.
Paris, Louvre.
This scene was part of the wall decoration of the mastaba of
Akhethetep, which consisted of everyday scenes of his life.
The tomb, built at Saqqara, has been reconstructed in the
Louvre.

Left: Seated statue of a man,
Vth Dynasty (2563–2423 B.C.*).*
Painted limestone, with inlaid eyes;
height 61 cm.
Cairo, Egyptian Museum.
This statue, representing an unknown
man wearing the ceremonial dress and
the wig, was found in the same Saqqara
tomb that contained the statue of the
scribe, now in the Egyptian Museum,
Cairo (see below).

Page 38: The Scribe,
Vth Dynasty (2563–2423 B.C.*).*
Painted limestone, with inlaid eyes
(white quartz, ebony and rock crystal);
height 53 cm.
Paris, Louvre.
This statue almost certainly represents
the provincial governor Kai in the
position of a scribe—sitting cross-legged
on the ground with the papyrus roll in his
lap. From the necropolis at Saqqara.

Page 39: The Scribe,
Vth Dynasty (2563–2423 B.C.*).*
Painted limestone, with inlaid eyes,
height 51 cm.
Cairo, Egyptian Museum.
This statue, which resembles the Louvre
Scribe *(see the illustration on page 38*
and the caption above), is that of an
unknown character. The custom of
representing the dead in their everyday
official clothes was already widespread in
fourth-century tombs.
From the necropolis at Saqqara.

Right: Kemked,
Vth Dynasty (2563–2423 B.C.*).*
Painted limestone, with inlaid eyes;
height 43 cm.
Cairo, Egyptian Museum.
The funerary priest Kemked is shown
kneeling with joined hands, a typically
royal position.
From the necropolis at Saqqara.

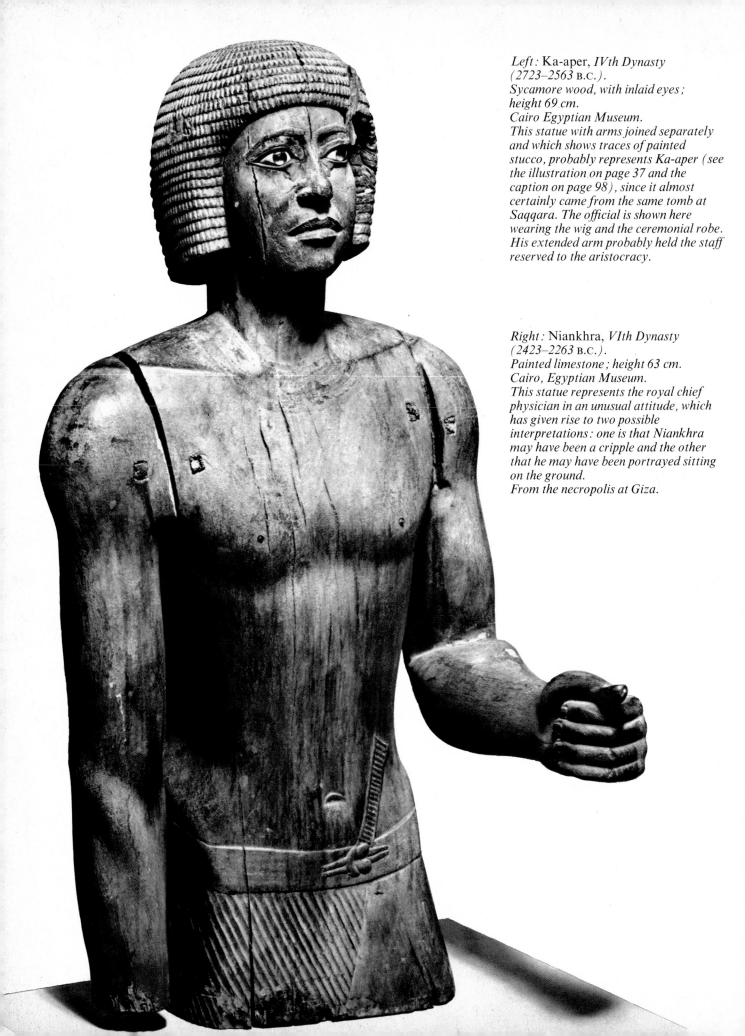

Left: Ka-aper, *IVth Dynasty
(2723–2563* B.C.*).
Sycamore wood, with inlaid eyes;
height 69 cm.
Cairo Egyptian Museum.
This statue with arms joined separately
and which shows traces of painted
stucco, probably represents Ka-aper (see
the illustration on page 37 and the
caption on page 98), since it almost
certainly came from the same tomb at
Saqqara. The official is shown here
wearing the wig and the ceremonial robe.
His extended arm probably held the staff
reserved to the aristocracy.*

Right: Niankhra, *VIth Dynasty
(2423–2263* B.C.*).
Painted limestone; height 63 cm.
Cairo, Egyptian Museum.
This statue represents the royal chief
physician in an unusual attitude, which
has given rise to two possible
interpretations: one is that Niankhra
may have been a cripple and the other
that he may have been portrayed sitting
on the ground.
From the necropolis at Giza.*

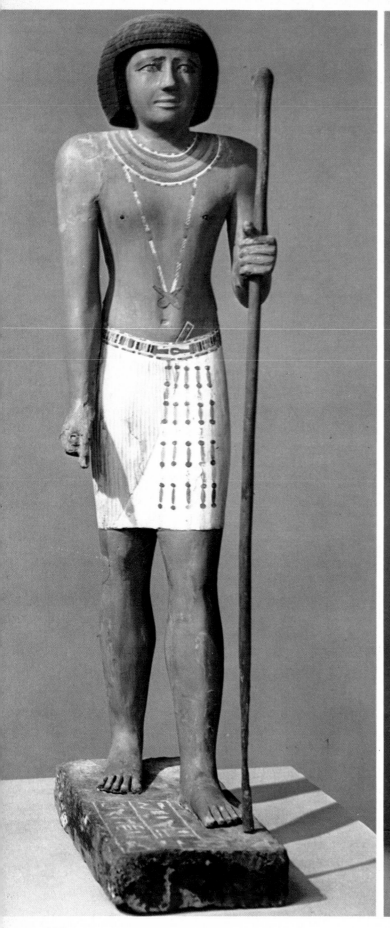

Page 108, left: Methethy,
Vth Dynasty (2563–2423 B.C.*).*
Wood covered with painted stucco;
height 89 cm.
New York, Brooklyn Museum.
The character portrayed in this statue is
shown holding in his left hand the staff of
aristocracy and in his right the sekhem
(now lost), the officials' scepter.

Page 108, right: Irukapta,
Vth Dynasty (2563–2423 B.C.*).*
Painted limestone;
height 73·5 cm.
New York, Brooklyn Museum.
The statue represents an official (as the
scepter held in the right hand indicates)
wearing the wig and the ceremonial robe.
The depiction of the family in a much
smaller size—the kneeling wife and the
son—is typical of the period.

Right (whole) and page 42
(detail): Husband and Wife,
Vth Dynasty (2563–2423 B.C.*).*
Wood; height of male figure 69 cm.;
height of female
figure 57·5 cm.
Paris, Louvre.
This work, which was originally covered
with stucco, portrays two unknown
characters; its origin, too, is unknown.
The scepter in the man's right hand
indicates that he was an official. The
woman has her left arm around her
husband. This type of wooden statue was
considered a magical substitute for the
dead persons and was used as such in
funerary ceremonies.

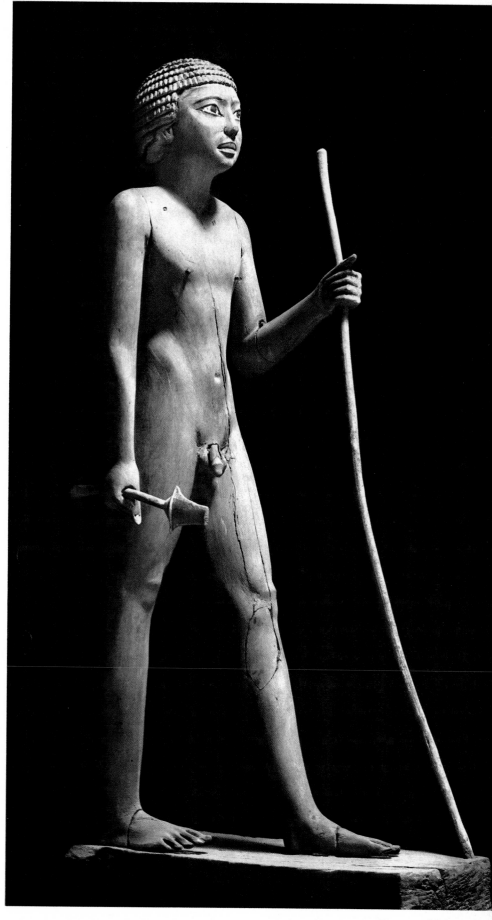

Left: Woman making beer,
Vth Dynasty (2563–2423 B.C.*).*
Painted terra cotta; height 26·7 cm.
Cairo, Egyptian Museum.
*This funerary ornament on the theme of
domestic work shows a woman crushing
in a jar barley and wheat, the two cereals
used by the Egyptians in making beer.*

Right: Statue of a man,
VIth Dynasty (2423–2263 B.C.*).*
Ebony wood; height 66 cm.
Cairo, Egyptian Museum.
*The character is shown holding the
aristocrat's staff and the* sekhem, *the
official's scepter. The fact that he is
represented in the nude is extremely
unusual because this was normally
reserved to children and adolescents
only. From the tomb of the master of
ceremonies Merire-hashtef, near
Herakleopolis.*

Above, The reviewing of livestock,
XIth Dynasty (2160–2000 B.C.).
Wood, covered with painted stucco;
length of base 175 cm.
Cairo, Egyptian Museum.
This funerary ornament comes from the
tomb of the chancellor Mekutra, at Deir
el Bahri, near Thebes. It shows
an everyday scene in the life
of an official, the reviewing of
his livestock.

Page 46: Fishing scene,
XIth Dynasty (2160–2000 B.C.).
Wood, covered with
painted stucco;
length of base 60 cm.
Cairo, Egyptian Museum.
This, too, comes from Mekutra's tomb.
It shows slaves fishing with nets
from papyrus boats. Their master
and other servants look on from
the two boats with baldaquins.

Above: Woman grinding corn,
Vth Dynasty (2563–2423 B.C.*).*
Painted limestone;
height c. *35 cm.*
Florence, Museo Archeologico.
This funerary statuette depicts a
domestic scene with amazing
realism.

Page 45: Woman bearing offerings,
XIIth Dynasty (2000–1785 B.C.*).*
Wood, covered with painted stucco; height 104 cm.
Paris, Louvre.
This funerary ornament shows a woman carrying food
offerings for the dead in their life beyond.
She balances on her head a basket containing a
haunch of beef and in her
right hand a libation vase.
From Assiut.

Left: Pharaoh Senwosret I
(1970–1936 B.C.*), XIIth Dynasty.*
Painted cedar wood, crown and
robe covered with plaster;
height 57 cm.
Cairo, Egyptian Museum.
The pharaoh is shown holding the staff of
command and wearing the crown of
Upper Egypt. The pendant of the statue
illustrated on page 116, this work was
probably used in the funerary rites for
the king's chancellor, Imhotep, in whose
tomb at Lisht they were both found.

Page 47: Pharaoh Nebhepetra
Mentuhotpe
(detail), XIth Dynasty
(2160–2000 B.C.*).*
Painted grey sandstone;
height 175 cm.
Cairo, Egyptian Museum.
This statue, which came from the king's
funerary temple at Deir el Bahri, is in an
excellent state of preservation, for it was
found wrapped up in bands like a
mummy. It almost certainly represents
Mentuhotpe I, fourth king of the XIth
Dynasty, and shows him wearing the red
crown of Lower Egypt and the jubilee
robe.

Right and page 44 (details):
Soldiers, IX–Xth Dynasty.
Wood covered with painted stucco;
height 40 cm.;
length of base 193 cm.
Cairo, Egyptian Museum.
This funerary ornament represents a unit
of forty Nubian soldiers armed with
pikes and shields and marching four
abreast. It is similar to a unit of archers
found in the tomb of Prince Mesekhti in
Assiut.

Left: Pharaoh Senwosret I
(1970–1936 B.C.*), XIIth Dynasty.*
Painted cedar wood, crown
and robe covered with plaster;
height 58·4 cm.
New York,
Metropolitan Museum of Art.
The king is shown holding the staff
of command and the crown of
Lower Egypt. The statue was the
pendant of the work shown on
page 114.
From the necropolis at Lisht.

Above: The Sphinx of Senwosret III
(1887–1850 B.C.*),*
XIIth Dynasty.
Granite; height 42·5 cm.;
length of base 73·5 cm.
New York,
Metropolitan Museum of Art.
The figure of the sphinx, which combines
the body of a lion with the head of
a man, symbolizes the royal status
of the pharaoh, to whom were
attributed the lion's physical and
moral force.

Page 48: Head of a woman,
XIIth Dynasty
(2000–1785 B.C.*).*
Wood; height 8·5 cm.
Cairo, Egyptian Museum.
This small head was
originally painted and had
inlaid eyes. It has
a large, removable wig
which was covered with
gold leaves, according
to the fashion of the
time.

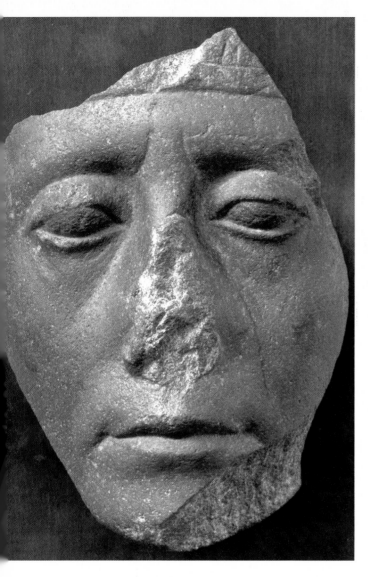

Left: Pharaoh Senwosret I
(1970–1936 B.C.*), XIIth Dynasty.*
White limestone; height 195 cm.
Cairo, Egyptian Museum.
The pharaoh is represented wearing
the ceremonial dress, the false beard, and
the linen headdress complete with
uraeus. Enclosed in his right
hand is the amulet which will give
him the strength to revive
after death. From Lisht.

Above, left: Pharaoh Senwosret III
(1887–1850 B.C.*),*
XIIth Dynasty.
Red quartzite;
height 16·5 cm.
New York,
Metropolitan Museum of Art.
This poorly preserved
head was probably a funerary
portrait of the pharaoh as an
old man.

Above, right: Pharaoh Amenemhat III
(1850–1800 B.C.*),*
XIIth Dynasty.
Grey granite; height 35 cm.
Cairo,
Egyptian Museum.
This head belonged to a now
lost statue. It represents
the pharaoh wearing the white
crown of Upper Egypt.
From Kom el Hisn.

Left: Pharaoh Amenemhat III
(1850–1800 B.C.*), XIIth Dynasty.*
Black granite; height 110 cm.
Cairo, Egyptian Museum.
The king is shown standing, with his left
leg forward, according to the traditional
attitude reserved to male statues. He is
wearing the ceremonial striped linen
headdress and the uraeus, *symbol of*
royalty. His name and titles are
inscribed on the socle, beside his feet.

Right: Pharaoh Amenemhat III
(1850–1800 B.C.*), XIIth Dynasty.*
Yellow limestone; height 160 cm.
Cairo, Egyptian Museum.
The king is shown seated on his throne,
wearing the ceremonial striped linen
headdress with the uraeus *and with an*
amulet around his neck. His name and
titles are inscribed on the throne.
From El Fayum.

Left: Sphinx of Amenemhat III
(1850–1800 B.C.), XIIth Dynasty.
Black granite; length of base 225 cm.
Cairo, Egyptian Museum.
The sphinx, a creature half-lion and half-man, was the
symbol of royalty, combining the strength of the lion with
the power of the king. This particular figure is one of four
sphinxes from Tanis. The fact that the creature sports a
mane instead of the usual linen headdress is probably due to
the Hyksos influence.

Above: Pharaoh Amenemhat III
(1850–1800 B.C.), XIIth Dynasty.
Black granite; height 100 cm.
Cairo, Egyptian Museum.
This fragment of a lost statue almost certainly represents
King Amenhotpe III. He is wearing unusual garb, found
only in this statue, and probably of a ritual nature—heavy
wig, ceremonial false beard, several necklaces, and two
badges with falcon heads.

Left: Figures bearing offerings
to the Nile, *XIIth Dynasty
(2000–1785* B.C.*).*
Grey granite; height 160 cm.
Cairo, Egyptian Museum.
*The figures probably represent the two
genies of the Nile, those of Upper and
Lower Egypt. The offerings platforms
before each of them hold a fish. More
fish and lotus flowers decorate the front
and sides of the platforms.*

Right: Queen Nefert *(detail),*
XIIth Dynasty (2000–1785 B.C.*).*
Black granite; height 165 cm.
Cairo, Egyptian Museum.
The wife of Senwosret II (1906–1888
B.C.*) is represented—wearing an unusual
headdress; it is similar to that of a
number of statues of Hathor, the great
mother goddess of the pharaohs.*
From Tanis.

Left: The Lady Sennui,
XIIth Dynasty (2000–1785 B.C.).
Black granite; height 168 cm.
Boston, Museum of Fine Arts.
Sennui is seated on a cube-shaped seat entirely inscribed with hieroglyphics giving her names and attributes. She is wearing a long dress and a wig; her right hand holds a flower, symbol of resurrection after death.
From Kerma.

Right: Hetep, *XIIth Dynasty (2000–1785 B.C.).*
Grey granite; height 74 cm.
Cairo, Egyptian Museum.
This is one of the first examples of the cubic statue, a type of work that illustrates in the round a subject matter already found in Old Kingdom reliefs—that of a man crouching in a seat, from which only the head, arms, and legs emerge. From the tomb of the treasurer Hetep at Saqqara, in which the artist imitated the style of the VIth Dynasty.

126

Left: The *ka* of Pharaoh Hor
(detail), c. *1800* B.C., *XIIth Dynasty.*
Gilded ebony; height 175 cm.
Cairo, Egyptian Museum.
This statue represents the ka, *or spiritual double, of the*
king. The two raised arms on its head are in the shape of
the hieroglyphic denoting this. From a tomb at Dahshur,
where it was found in a gilded wood shrine.

Right: Sahathor, *XIIth Dynasty (2000–1785* B.C.*).*
Painted limestone; height 40·6 cm.
London, British Museum.
The treasurer Sahathor is represented as a "cubic statue,"
with his head, arms, and feet emerging. From Abydos,
where other such statues were used as votive offerings in
the temple of Osiris.

130

Left: Queen Tetisheri,
XVIIIth Dynasty
(1580–1314 B.C.*).*
Painted limestone; height 37 cm.
London, British Museum.
The simplicity of the treatment
of this statuette is due to the fact
that it was dedicated to the queen's
memory by one of her descendants
during the reign of her son Ahmose
(1580–1558 B.C.*).*

Above: Sphinx of Queen
Hatshepsut *(1505–1484* B.C.*),*
XVIIIth Dynasty.
Limestone; height 61 cm.
New York,
Metropolitan Museum of Art.
The sphinx's face is that of
Queen Hatshepsut, and added to it are
the lion's mane and the ceremonial
false beard.
From Deir el Bahri.

Page 49: Pharaoh Thutmose I
(1530–1520 B.C.*),*
XVIIIth Dynasty.
Painted limestone; height 120 cm.
Cairo, Egyptian Museum.
This is a fragment of a colossal
statue showing the pharaoh wrapped
in a mantle. With other similar
statues it adorned the
pilasters in a corridor of the
temple at Karnak.

Left : Group of slaves, rowing
(15th century B.C.*), XVIIIth Dynasty.*
Bas-relief, painted limestone ;
height c. *40 cm.*
Berlin, Staatliche Museen.
This fragment of a wall decoration represents a
scene of everyday life. It was found in the tomb of
Pharaoh Thutmose III (1504–1450 B.C.*) at Deir*
el Bahri.

Right : Pharaoh Amenhotpe II
*(*c. *1450–1425* B.C.*),*
XVIIIth Dynasty.
Grey granite ; height 123 cm.
Cairo, Egyptian Museum.
This new way of depicting pharaohs shows them
kneeling, and holding a tablet with offerings
before them. In this example, one of the oldest of
its kind, the pharaoh is shown wearing the
ceremonial garb. The offerings are symbolized by
two-dimensional engravings on the surface of the
tablet.
From Karnak.

Left: Pharaoh Amenhotpe II
(c. 1450–1425 B.C.),
XVIIIth Dynasty.
Pink granite; height 152 cm.
Turin, Museo Egizio.
The pharaoh is shown kneeling in the
ritual position and offering two jars of
wine to the gods.
From Thebes.

Right: Head of a King,
XVIIIth Dynasty
(1580–1314 B.C.).
Obsidian; height 18 cm.
Cairo, Egyptian Museum.
This fragment of a statue originally had
inlaid eyes and a crown, probably of
gold.
From Karnak.

Left : Pharaoh Thutmose IV
and his mother, Queen Tiy
(c. 1425–1408 B.C.), XVIIIth Dynasty.
Black granite ; height 110 cm.
Cairo, Egyptian Museum.
The subject matter of two seated statues
presented as a couple but nevertheless
separate had already been treated in the
Fourth Dynasty. It is developed here in a
homogeneous way which was to have a
great vogue. The two sitters hold each
other by the waist. The pharaoh's bare
feet rest on the "nine bows," symbol of
Egypt's supremacy over her enemies.
The sitters are traditionally dressed,
except for the fact that the king is
wearing a civilian wig, which he
apparently favoured.
From Karnak.

Right : Pharaoh Thutmose III
(1504–1450 B.C.),
XVIIIth Dynasty.
Grey basalt ; height 200 cm.
Cairo, Egyptian Museum.
The pharaoh is wearing the
white crown of Upper Egypt
and ceremonial dress.
From Karnak.

Left: Pharaoh Amenhotpe III
(1408–1372 B.C.*),*
XVIIIth Dynasty.
Black granite; height 240 cm.
London, British Museum.
The pharaoh is shown seated on his
throne wearing ceremonial dress, with
the false beard and the nemes—*the*
striped linen headdress—adorned with
the uraeus.

Page 50: The Goddess Hathor
and Pharaoh Amenhotpe II
(c. 1450–1425 B.C.*),*
XVIIIth Dynasty.
Painted limestone;
length of base 225 cm.
Cairo, Egyptian Museum.
This symbolic representation of Hathor,
the heifer goddess, who personified Isis
and looked after the dead, is in
accordance with the ancient Egyptian
beliefs about life beyond the grave. The
dead, following the sun (the solar disc is
held between the heifer's horns), go and
live on the Western Mountain, past the
swamps where papyrus grows (shown on
the sculpture beside the heifer's
shoulders). The pharaoh is portrayed
either before the heifer, under her
protection (as is the case here), or
beneath her as she suckles him, thereby
infusing him with new life beyond death.
From the sanctuary at Deir el Bahri
dedicated to the goddess Hathor by
Thutmose III, father of Amenhotpe II.

Right: Pharaoh Thutmose IV
(c. 1425–1408 B.C.*),*
XVIIIth Dynasty.
Bronze; height 14·2 cm.
London, British Museum.
The pharaoh is shown offering
the ritual wine jars.

Above: Head of a Queen
(14th century B.C.), XVIIIth Dynasty.
Grey granite; height 50 cm.
Cairo, Egyptian Museum.
This fragment of a statue almost
certainly represents Queen Tiy, wife of
Amenhotpe III (1408–1372 B.C.).
She is wearing a heavy wig adorned
by a diadem with a vulture, symbol
of Nekhebet, the patron goddess
of the dynasty from Upper Egypt.

Page 51: Pharaoh Akhenaton
and Queen Nafertiti
(1372–1354 B.C.),
XVIIIth Dynasty.
Painted limestone; height 22·5 cm.
Paris, Louvre.
The king and his wife,
wearing everyday clothes
(with sandals but the
blue ceremonial crown), are
shown holding hands.

Right: Pharaoh Amenhotpe III
and his family
(1408–1372 B.C.),
XVIIIth Dynasty.
Limestone; height 7 m.
Cairo, Egyptian Museum.
This colossal group represents
Amenhotpe III, his wife Tiy, and three of
their children (only two are shown
in the illustration).
From Medinet Habu.

140

Left: Pharaoh Akhenaton
(1372–1354 B.C.*), XVIIIth Dynasty.*
Painted limestone with alabaster socle;
height 40 cm.
Cairo, Egyptian Museum.
The king, wearing ceremonial dress, is
holding an offerings tablet engraved with
food and flowers. Although he is wearing
the blue ceremonial crown, his sandals
are part of everyday dress. The feet held
close together and the golden colour of
the skin are elements usually reserved to
female portraits.
From Tell el' Amarna.

Page 52: Pharaoh Smenkhara *(detail)*
(1372–1354 B.C.*), XVIIIth Dynasty.*
Yellow steatite; height 61 cm.
Paris, Louvre.
This statue shows the pharaoh wearing
ceremonial dress, with the linen
headdress and the scepter. Smenkhara
was the brother and son-in-law of
Akhenaton and his co-ruler in the last
years of his reign.

Page 53: Queen Nafertiti
(14th century B.C.*),*
XVIIIth Dynasty.
Painted limestone; height 50 cm.
Berlin, Staatliche Museen.
The queen is wearing the blue crown
that no other queen is known to
have worn.
From Tell el' Amarna.

Page 54: Queen Nafertiti
(14th century B.C.*),*
XVIIIth Dynasty.
Partly painted quartzite;
height 33 cm.
Cairo, Egyptian Museum.
This unfinished head, found in a
sculptor's workshop at Tell el' Amarna,
still bears traces of colour on the
forehead, eyes, and along the nose, which
were probably working marks made by
the sculptor. Once finished, it would
probably have had a wig or a crown.

Right: The Goddess Mut (detail),
XVIIIth Dynasty, (1580–1314 B.C.*)*
Limestone; height 140 cm.
Cairo, Egyptian Museum.
Mut, wife of the god Amun and female
deity of the Karnak region, is depicted
wearing a wig and a very high crown
(not shown in the illustration).

Left: Pharaoh Akhenaton
(1372–1354 B.C.*),*
XVIIIth Dynasty.
Stucco; height 24 cm.
Berlin, Staatliche Museen.
This head, found in a sculptor's
workshop at Tell el'Amarna, was
probably part of a composite statue, one
made of different materials.

Page 55: A daughter of Akhenaton,
XVIIIth Dynasty (1580–1314 B.C.*).*
Partly painted quartzite;
height 21 cm.
Cairo, Egyptian Museum.
This unfinished little head from Tell el
'Amarna still bears traces of colour,
which were probably guide marks for the
sculptor. The features resemble
Akhenaton's (1372–1354 B.C.*).*

Page 56: An Amarna princess,
XVIIIth Dynasty (1580–1314 B.C.*).*
Painted limestone;
height 15·5 cm.
Paris, Louvre.
This little bust probably represents a
royal child—the asymmetrical wig was
worn only by children. The pleated dress
and large breastplate (of which few
traces remain) seem to indicate that she
was wearing ceremonial dress, which is
unusual because Egyptian children
normally went about naked.

Right: Pharaoh Akhenaton
(1372–1354 B.C.*),*
XVIIIth Dynasty.
Painted sandstone; height 4 m.
Cairo, Egyptian Museum.
With about thirty similar statues, this
colossal statue of Akhenaton used to
adorn the pillars in a court of the Temple
of Amun at Karnak. The pharaoh is
wearing royal dress, with a double crown
over a small nemes, *or linen headdress,*
and he is holding two scepters crossed
over his breast.

Right: Walking in a garden.
XVIIIth Dynasty (1580–1314 B.C.*).*
Bas-relief, painted limestone;
height 25·4 cm.;
length of base 21 cm.
Berlin, Staatliche Museen.
The characters are possibly Smenkhara,
brother of and co-ruler with Akhenaton
(1372–1354 B.C.*), and his wife*
Meritaton, who was also his niece.
From Giza.

Opposite: Head of a man,
XVIIIth Dynasty (1580–1314 B.C.*).*
Painted wood; height 20 cm.
Paris, Louvre.
This little head was part of the
decoration of a harp.
From Tell el ʿAmarna.

Below: Negro prisoners,
XVIIIth Dynasty (1580–1314 B.C.*).*
Bas-relief, limestone;
length of base 82 cm.
Bologna, Museo Civico.
This panel came from the tomb that
General Haremhab ordered built for
himself at Saqqara, before he became
pharaoh (1344–1314 B.C.*). The subject*
matter of the relief is the presentation of
prisoners of war to Akhenaton.

Left: The God Amun and the Pharaoh Tutankhamun *(detail)* *(c. 1354–1340 B.C.), XVIIIth Dynasty. Black granite; height 220 cm. Paris, Louvre.* The group represents Amun, the god of air, protecting the pharaoh. The detail shown here shows the god's face in profile, with the ceremonial false beard and breastplate and the beginning of his very high crown in the shape of two feathers.

Page 57: Pharaoh Tutankhamun *(c. 1354–1340 B.C.), XVIIIth Dynasty. Gilded and painted wood; height 204 cm. Cairo, Egyptian Museum.* This is a detail of the king's second sarcophagus found in his provisional tomb in the Valley of the Kings. He is wearing the linen nemes, *with its coloured stripes, surmounted by the symbols of the patron goddesses of Upper Egypt (Nekhebet, personified by a vulture) and Lower Egypt (Wadjet, personified by the* uraeus*)*.

Page 58: The Goddess Neith, *XVIIIth Dynasty (1580–1314 B.C.). Gilded and painted wood; height 78·1 cm. Cairo, Egyptian Museum.* This is a detail of the "Canopic chest," the large (200 × 125 × 153 cm.) chest of gilded wood in which the king's viscera were kept. It was found in the tomb of Tutankhamun *(c. 1354–1340 B.C.). The statues of Neith and three other goddesses—Isis, Nephthys, and Selkis— were placed against the four panels of the chest to protect the royal viscera.*

Right: Pharaoh Tutankhamun *(c. 1354–1340 B.C.), XVIIIth Dynasty. Granite; height 157 cm. Cairo, Egyptian Museum.* This detail shows the pharaoh's face framed by the linen headdress with its coloured stripes and the uraeus.

Left: Sennefer and his family,
XVIIIth Dynasty (1580–1314 B.C.*)*.
Black granite; height 120 cm.
Cairo, Egyptian Museum.
*Sennefer, governor of Thebes at the
time of Amenhotpe II (*c. *1450–1425*
B.C.*), is represented in this typical
family group, with his wife and
daughter depicted, as usual, in much
smaller dimensions. Sennefer's
numerous gold necklaces indicate his
exalted position. The names and
qualifications of the couple are
inscribed in a narrow strip on their
skirts.*
From Karnak.

Right: Nebsen and Nebetta,
*XVIIIth Dynasty
(1580–1314* B.C.*)*.
*Painted limestone;
height 40·4 cm.*
New York, Brooklyn Museum.
*This commemorative group
represents a scribe of the royal
treasury and of the temple of Amun,
with his wife.*

Left: Amenhotpe son of Hapy,
XVIIIth Dynasty
(1580–1314 B.C.*).*
Black granite; height 117 cm.
Cairo, Egyptian Museum.
Amenhotpe, the architect and counsellor
of King Amenhotpe III (1408–1372
B.C.*), is represented as a young scribe.*
This, together with the statue on the
opposite page, came from the temple of
Amun at Karnak.

Page 59: Pharaoh Tutankhamun
(c. 1354–1340 B.C.*),*
XVIIIth Dynasty.
Stuccoed and painted wood,
with inlaid eyes; height 42 cm.
Cairo, Egyptian Museum.
Because of the unusual armless and
naked bust, this statue has been placed
among other similar works which must
have been private portraits of the dead
used in funerary rites.
From Tutankhamun's tomb in the
Valley of the Kings.

Page 60: Small royal head.
XVIIIth Dynasty
(1580–1314 B.C.*).*
Glass paste; height 9·3 cm.
Paris, Louvre.
The head bears a crown from which the
frontal uraeus *is lost. The eyes were*
probably inlaid.

Right: Amenhotpe son of Hapy,
XVIIIth Dynasty (1580–1314 B.C.*).*
Grey granite; height 142 cm.
Cairo, Egyptian Museum.
The architect of Amenhotpe III is
represented here as an old scribe of
eighty (in later tradition he became a
god of wisdom). Like the statue on the
opposite page, this came from the temple
of Amun at Karnak.

Left: Portrait of a lady,
*XVIIIth Dynasty
(1580–1314* B.C.*).
Limestone; height 50·5 cm.
Florence, Museo Archeologico.
This fragment of a statue portrays an
aged lady wearing the long wig
characteristic of the late XVIIIth
Dynasty.*

Page 61: The Lady Nai,
*XIXth Dynasty
(1314–1200* B.C.*).
Partly gilded wood;
height 26·5 cm.
Paris, Louvre.
This statuette was a funerary portrait
destined to be placed in a tomb. The
dress and heavy wig are
characteristically Theban.*

Right: The Lady Tui *(detail),
XVIII–XIXth Dynasty
(14th–13th century* B.C.*).
Acacia wood; height 33 cm.
Paris, Louvre.
Like other Theban ladies of her time, Tui
performed religious functions. The left
hand, at her breast, holds the* menant,
*the necklace denoting her rank of
priestess.*

Left: Pharaoh Ramesses II
(1301–1235 B.C.*),*
XIXth Dynasty.
Black granite; height 194 cm.
Turin, Museo Egizio.
Seated on a low-backed, cube-shaped throne, the pharaoh is represented wearing the ceremonial dress with the blue crown and the long-sleeved pleated tunic with a shawl. Hieroglyphics inscribed on the tunic give the king's name and his divine titles. He holds the scepter in his right hand and in his left a stylized version of the ancient staff of the aristocracy. The king's feet rest on the "nine bows" engraved on the socle, which symbolize the enemies of Egypt. Leaning against the throne, next to the pharaoh's legs, are the much smaller figures of his wife, Nafertari, and one of his sons.
From Karnak.

Page 63: Pharaoh Ramesses II
(1301–1235 B.C.*),*
XIXth Dynasty.
Grey granite; height 77 cm.
Cairo, Egyptian Museum.
This fragment of a very large statue represents the king wearing the uraeus-bearing *wig and the ceremonial dress consisting of a long-sleeved pleated tunic with a pleated shawl on the left shoulder. His right hand, against his chest, holds the scepter.*
From Tanis.

Right: Pharaoh Ramesses II
and the falcon-headed god Horus
(1301–1235 B.C.*), XIXth Dynasty.*
Grey granite; height 210 cm.
Cairo, Egyptian Museum.
The king is represented as a child, crouching under the protection of the falcon-headed god Horus, father of the pharaohs, who is incarnated in him. On the child's characteristic asymmetrical wig is placed the solar disc, symbol of Hathor, the divine mother of the pharaohs. The child holds in his hands a rush and a bee, the respective symbols of Upper and Lower Egypt.

Left: A princess of Ramesses's family,
*XIXth Dynasty (1314–1200 B.C.).
Painted limestone; height 75 cm.
Cairo, Egyptian Museum.*
The princess's long wig is encircled by a
diadem bearing the two frontal uraeuses
(with the symbols of Upper and Lower
Egypt) and topped by a crown made of
uraeuses *enclosing the solar disc. The
princess is also wearing earrings,
bracelets, and a breastplate. She is
holding in her left hand a jewel which she
would shake as the pharaoh went by.
This fragment of a statue comes from
Ramesses II's (1301–1235 B.C.)
funerary temple at Karnak.*

Page 62: Tchai,
*XIXth Dynasty (1314–1200 B.C.).
Sudanese ebony; height 41 cm.
Cairo, Egyptian Museum.
This funerary portrait represents an
official; he is holding in his right hand
the scepter reserved to those with
governing functions. The long pleated
tunic with sleeves and the shorter wig are
the characteristic garb of the New
Kingdom.
From Saqqara.*

Right: Pharaoh Ramesses VI
*(post-1156 B.C.),
XXth Dynasty.
Grey granite; height 74 cm.
Cairo, Egyptian Museum.
The king is represented dressed for war,
with the crown of Osiris, an ax, and the
head of an enemy.
From Karnak.*

View of the funerary temple
of Pharaoh Ramesses II
(1301–1235 B.C.),
XIXth Dynasty.
Limestone ; height of the colossi 20 m.
Abu Simbel (Nubia).
The entrance to the temple, carved out of
a rock above the river Nile, is adorned by
the four colossal statues of the gods that
were worshipped there—Amun of
Thebes ; Ra-Harakhty of Heliopolis ;
Ptah of Memphis ; and the pharaoh
himself in the shape of a god. The temple
was transferred to a higher spot in the
early 1960s, to prevent its being flooded
by the waters of the Aswan Dam.

160

Left: Thai and Nai *(detail),*
XIXth Dynasty
(1314–1200 B.C.).
Limestone; height 90 cm.
Cairo, Egyptian Museum.
Husband and wife are seated
on a high-backed chair.
Although the clothes and wigs
are characteristic of the
late XVIIIth Dynasty, the work
is of a slightly later date.
From the necropolis at Saqqara.

Above: Ramesses III hunting the wild bull
(1198–1166 B.C.), XXth Dynasty.
Bas-relief, painted limestone; height c. 250 cm.
Temple of Medinet Habu.
In this complex composition the traditional
arrangement in narrative strips is only partly
maintained. The central episode is asymmetrically
depicted: the pharaoh in his chariot is hunting
wild bulls under the protection of the falcon-headed
god Horus. The strips below are
engraved with archers and
hieroglyphics.

Left: Naia and Mut-Nefer,
XIXth Dynasty (1314–1200 B.C.).
Painted limestone; height 54 cm.
Munich, Staatliche
Sammheng Agyptischer Kunst.
This funerary group represents Naia,
a priest of Amun, with his mother, as
indicated by the hieroglyphics inscribed on
their clothes and the base of the
statues. From a tomb in Thebes, as
indicated by the inscription.

Above: The God Thoth and the Scribe Nebmertuf,
XIXth Dynasty
(1314–1200 B.C.).
Schist; height 19·4 cm.
Paris, Louvre.
The scribe is shown sitting
beside a small shrine on which
is the effigy of the
baboon-headed god Thoth, protector
of writing, languages, laws, and
annals (and therefore of scribes).

165

Above: Mentuemhet *(detail)*,
XXVth Dynasty (751–656 B.C.).
Black granite; height 50 cm.
Cairo, Egyptian Museum.
This Ethiopian prince, who was
governor of Thebes under the last three
pharaohs of the dynasty, is
represented bare-headed.
From the temple of Mut at Karnak.

Right: Ramessesnakht,
XXth Dynasty.
Schist; height 40·5 cm.
Cairo, Egyptian Museum.
The high priest of Amun under Ramesses
IV (1166–1160 B.C.) is shown kneeling
before a shrine on which is placed the effigy
of the Theban triad: the god Amun with his
wife, Mut, and their son, Khonsu.

166

Left: Takushit,
XXVth Dynasty
(751–656 B.C.*).*
Bronze, inlaid with silver;
height 69 cm.
Athens, National Archeological Museum.
The woman portrayed in this
statuette (of funerary use) was
perhaps a priestess.

Page 64: Queen Karomama *(detail),*
XXIInd Dynasty.
Bronze, inlaid with gold;
height 59 cm.
Paris, Louvre.
The queen, wife of Pharaoh Takelot II
(847–823 B.C.*), is represented wearing a*
long pleated dress and a breastplate, and
the wig bearing the uraeus. *Her hips and*
legs are wrapped in the wings of the
falcon-headed god Horus; the feathers
were originally covered in gold plate.
The unusual position of the arms
indicates that she was probably holding
some object connected with the worship
of Amun. Like the other queens of her
dynasty, Karomama was a priestess of
Amun.

Right: Mentuemhet *(detail),*
end of the XXVth Dynasty
or beginning of the XXVIth
(mid-7th century B.C.*).*
Grey granite; height 135 cm.
Cairo, Egyptian Museum.
The governor of Thebes is
shown here in the traditional
pose of standing male statues,
holding in his hands
the scepters of command.
From Thebes.

Left: The Goddess Hathor and the Courtier Psamtik, *XXXth Dynasty (378–341* B.C.*).* *Green schist; height 79 cm.* *Cairo, Egyptian Museum.* *This group is a slightly simplified version of a traditional theme, that of the divine mother of the pharaohs and goddess of the dead protecting her son the pharaoh (see also pages 50 and 138). The character here, however, is a courtier and not a king. From the tomb of Psamtik at Saqqara.*

Right: Princess Amenarteis *(detail), XXVth Dynasty (751–656* B.C.*).* *Alabaster; height 167 cm.* *Cairo, Egyptian Museum.* *The princess is wearing the intricate wig used by the Ramessid princesses, with the falcon wings framing the face and the diadem of* uraeuses. *In her left hand, resting on her breast, she holds the whip-like scepter.* *From Karnak.*

Opposite, left: The Goddess
Thueris, *XXVIth Dynasty
(663–525* B.C.*).
Green schist; height 96 cm.
Cairo, Egyptian Museum.
Thueris, goddess of fertility
and patron goddess of
women in labour, was personified
by the hippopotamus, a very ancient
symbol of pacific power. She is
represented here leaning
on two "magic knots," a common
form of amulet.*

Opposite, right: Torso of
Pharaoh Hakor *(390–378* B.C.*),
XXIXth Dynasty.
Granite; height 180 cm.
Boston, Museum of Fine Arts.
This fragment of a colossal
statue shows King Hakor,
who liberated Egypt
from the Persian invaders,
in the traditional pose,
with his arms at his
sides and holding in his fists
the scepters of command.*

Above: Making lily ointment
*(detail), Ptolemaic period
(331–31* B.C.*).
Bas-relief, limestone:
height 31·5 cm.; length
of base 60 cm.
Turin, Museo Egizio.
Two women are using
sticks to squeeze the
piece of gauze containing
lilies, to collect the juice
which will make perfumed
ointment.*

A king of Meroe,
c. *100* B.C.
Sandstone; height 223 cm.
Copenhagen,
Ny Carlsberg Glyptotek.
This colossus, with other similar
statues, used to adorn the pilasters of
the temple of Isis at Meroe. One of
the Ethiopian kings of Meroe is
shown dressed in Egyptian clothes
(the uraeus *on his headdress, the*
breastplate, the short pleated skirt).

NOTES

GEOGRAPHICAL EXTENT

Several times during its very long history ancient Egypt extended its frontiers, was divided and reunified. As a geographical entity, though, it remained fixed throughout all its political changes by the areas on either side of the Nile, which were made fertile by the silt left behind every year after the flooding of the river, and irrigated by an intricate system of canals which had been established in very ancient times. In this largely desert country only the Nile valley and a few oases (Siwa, El Fayum, Kharga) were inhabitable.

The Old Kingdom began with the unification of Upper and Lower Egypt and eventually also included part of Nubia down to the Second Cataract. Its first capital was Abydos (close to the modern El Baliana), then Memphis (near present-day Cairo). Administratively the country was divided into provinces, called *nomoi*, and each of these had a capital. At the end of this period, after the rebellion of the Nubian mercenaries who guarded the frontiers, Nubia became independent.

During the Middle Kingdom Nubia was once more annexed, this time by King Senwosret III; then once again it was lost and Egypt itself was divided into a northern kingdom, whose capital was Tanis (near the modern San el Hagar), and a southern kingdom, whose capital was Thebes (near Luxor). The country was eventually reunified by one of the last pharaohs of the Middle Kingdom, then once again dismembered by the Hyksos invasions. The Hyksos moved their capital to the Delta, at Avaris (which may be Tanis).

The New Kingdom started with the reunification of Egypt, which now extended its power to include Syria, up to the Euphrates. Amenhotpe IV (Akhenaton) moved the capital to Tell el 'Amarna (known at the time as Akhetaton, the City of Aton), but Tutankhamun later moved it back to Thebes.

During the following period Egypt lost its Asian empire and was once more divided into two kingdoms, the Upper and the Lower, with Thebes and Tanis as capitals. A new reunification, by the Ethiopian king Piankhi, then took place, followed by the Assyrian conquest of Middle and Lower Egypt. A centralized monarchy was established after that by the princes of the city of Sais (the modern San el Hagar), which became the capital. At that time a canal was built to link the Mediterranean with the Red Sea through the isthmus of Suez. Annexed to Persia by King Cambyses II, Egypt eventually rebelled into independence. There was a second Persian conquest, then in 332 B.C. Egypt was finally conquered by Alexander the Great, who built himself a new capital, Alexandria. After his death Egypt was ruled by the Ptolemies (until the Roman occupation), whose kingdom, however, did not extend even to the Second Cataract. A new state was proclaimed in Nubia.

CHRONOLOGY

Old Kingdom (c. 3000–2263 B.C., I–VIth Dynasty)

I–IIIrd Dynasty: Menes Narmer, the first pharaoh, brings about the unification of Upper and Lower Egypt. The capital is Abydos. Memphis is founded. III–IVth Dynasty: Zoser moves the capital to Memphis. The architect Imhotep builds the first pyramid. The canon for sculpture is established. Policy of expansion, above all towards

Votive tablet of Pharaoh Narmer, 1st Dynasty (c. 3000 B.C.); back view. Cairo, Egyptian Museum (also see p. 13).

Nubia. The official worship is of the god Ra. Cheops, Chephren, and Mycerinus have the Giza pyramids built (IVth Dynasty). Gradual rise to power of the priests and heads (nomarchs) of the various provinces.

First Intermediate Period (c. 2263–2000 B.C., VII–Xth Dynasty)

Decline of centralized power; the country is decimated by civil wars. General economic and artistic decline.

Middle Kingdom (c. 2160–1680 B.C., XI–XVIth Dynasty)

The pharaohs of the XIth Dynasty bring about the reunification of the country. Trade with Nubia and the Red Sea countries is reestablished. The Theban god Amun is officially worshipped. Egypt loses Nubia and is again divided into two kingdoms which are eventually reunited by the pharaoh Sekhemre Sewadjitaui.

Hyksos invasions and Second Intermediate Period (c. 1730–1580 B.C., XV–XVIIth Dynasty)

The XVth and XVIth dynasties have a Hyksos counterpart. The official divinity is Seth. The pharaohs of the XVIIth Dynasty try to reunify the country.

New Kingdom (c. 1580–1085 B.C., XVIII–XXth Dynasty)

Under the XVIIIth Dynasty Egypt has its golden age. The cult of Amun is reinstated. Amenhotpe I, Thutmose III, Queen Hatshepsut, Amenhotpe III consolidate the power of the pharaohs. The great temple compounds of Deir el Bahri, Luxor, and Karnak are built. Amenhotpe IV, changing his name to Akhenaton, imposes, together with his wife Nafertiti, the monotheistic cult of Aton, as opposed to Amun. The successor of Tutankhamun reestablishes the ancient cults. XIXth Dynasty: Ramesses II conquers Syria and wins a great victory against the Hittites at Kadesh (1299 B.C.). XXth Dynasty:

Ramesses III is victorious after a long war with the People from the Sea (among them the Cretans and the Achaeans). The country is torn by internal strife because of the tug of war between politics and religion.

Low Epoch (c. 1085–30 B.C.)

Third Intermediate Period (c. 1085–663 B.C., XXI–XXVth Dynasty)

A restless period during which many kings reigned, some of them simultaneously. The XXVth Dynasty is Ethiopian. The Assyrian invasion, headed by Ashurbanipal, puts an end to the period.

Saitic monarchy (c. 663–525 B.C., XXVIth Dynasty)

Twenty-sixth Dynasty founded by the princes of Sais. Psamtik I repels the Assyrian invaders. Necho I begins construction of a canal across the isthmus of Suez and directs Phoenician sailors to sail right around Africa.

First Persian occupation (c. 525–404 B.C., XXVIIth Dynasty)

Cambyses, king of Persia, conquers Egypt and founds a new dynasty.

Last Egyptian dynasties (c. 404–341 B.C., XXVIII–XXXth Dynasty)

The struggle against the Persians continues, in many cases, with the alliance of some of the Greek city states.

Second Persian occupation (c. 341–332 B.C.)

In 333 B.C. Alexander the Great routs Darius III, Persian emperor. In 332 he occupies Egypt.

Greek period (c. 332–30 B.C.)

One of Alexander's lieutenants, Ptolemy, founds a new dynasty in Alexandria, which becomes the capital of Egypt. Under the Ptolemies there is a new period of economic prosperity and flowering of the arts. The Ptolemaic dynasty remained in power until the Roman conquest of Egypt in 30 B.C.

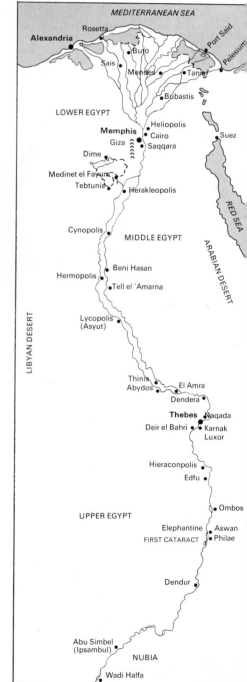

176

RELIGION

The complex structure of Egyptian religion is probably due to the fact that it was founded on a series of beliefs to which the prehistoric populations who inhabited the banks of the Nile already subscribed and which were added to for thousands of years. This was probably also responsible for the markedly local character of the cults; later the priests who tried to unify these cults into a national religion were compelled to take this character into account. With time, the Egyptians lost the precise sense of their own religious symbols (which were fiercely guarded by the priests) and were content to ask for the blessing of the gods in their daily life. Nature, of course, was the base for their religion, just as it was for their artistic and architectural concepts; the temples faced whichever way was determined by the surrounding natural context, and this context was reflected in their decoration.

The Heliopolis cosmogony was extremely ancient: *Atum,* the self-made god who emerged from the ocean onto the hill of Heliopolis, became the first god. He was later merged with the sun god, Ra. Atum-Ra begot *Shu,* the god of air and light, and *Tefnut,* goddess of the dew and the abyss. Shu and Tefnut begot *Geb,* the god of earth, and *Nut,* the goddess of the sky. Geb and Nut begot two sons, *Osiris* and *Seth,* and two daughters, *Isis* and *Neftis.* All these deities made up the great Heliopolis pantheon. Later *Horus,* son of Isis and Osiris, was added. The myths of the murder of Osiris by Seth say that his body was cut into pieces which were dispersed throughout Egypt. Isis succeeded in finding them all and reconstructing the body of Osiris, making him live again and conceiving Horus, who avenged his father's murder. Other divinities worshipped at Heliopolis included *Thoth,* patron of scribes, *Maat,* goddess of truth, and *Anubis,* god of travel.

The Memphis cosmogony developed after Memphis became the capital of unified Egypt. At its center was the god *Ptah,* patron of craftsmen and artists. It was said that he begot eight other Ptahs in order to form the Ennead. The sun, too, was said to have been born of an egg created by Ptah. It is interesting to note that in the Hermopolis cosmogony, too, the sun god came out of an egg on the hill of Hermopolis and then started to give shape and order to the universe. As in other civilizations, there was also the guardian spirit of tombs or temples, the Sphinx, that drew its power from the combination of several different natures.

The importance of these various cults was intimately dependent on the political importance of their centers. Among the many triads, consisting of one national god and two minor local divinities, was that of Thebes; it consisted of *Amun-Ra* as the central figure, his wife *Mut,* the sky goddess with the face of a vulture, and their son *Khonsu,* god of the moon. The Egyptian religion being much influenced by nature, this was reflected in the personification of its various gods. *Ra* has different personifications; *Ra-Horus* is personified by a man with the head of a falcon; *Horus,* however, the avenger of his father, is usually represented by a child sitting on a throne; when he is shown as god of the sky, he is personified by a man with the sun and the moon instead of eyes; as the protector of the pharaohs, he is represented by a falcon. *Shu* and his sister *Tefnut* are symbolized by lions. *Geb* is a man stretched out under the vault of heaven, and *Nut* is often represented above him as a woman with a star-strewn body, curved like the heavens, but with her hands and feet touching the earth. *Osiris* is represented by a shrouded man with a crown on his head and folded arms, holding the staff and whip. *Seth,* personification of evil, is often represented by an unidentifiable animal akin to a wolf or a jackal;

Above: The Great Sphinx and the pyramid of Chephren at Giza, IVth Dynasty (2723–2563 B.C.*). Top: The step pyramid and funerary temple of Zoser at Saqqara, IIIrd Dynasty (2778–2723* B.C.*).*

sometimes also as a pig, a donkey, or a hippopotamus. *Isis* is dressed as a woman, but with a throne-shaped headdress; she is usually shown weeping (like her sister *Neftis*); later, however, she is represented suckling her son, Horus. *Thoth* is personified by a dog- or ibis-headed man. *Maat* is a woman wearing a headdress made of an ostrich feather. *Anubis* is a dog, or a dog-headed man, or a jackal-headed man. *Hapy*, the sacred bull of Memphis, bears the solar disc held between its horns, and sometimes a triangle on its forehead.

The cult of the dead occupied a central position in Egyptian religious life. Since it was necessary for the body to be preserved if it were ever to attain immortality as the embodiment of Osiris, the technique of mummification was developed and perfected. The mummy, whose mouth was open symbolically, was brought food and wine, for it was believed that life went on after death. The tombs were therefore filled with objects of daily use: jewels, amulets, vases, ornaments of all sorts. During the New Kingdom the custom was introduced of placing in the coffin a roll of papyrus with religious and magic texts, mostly from the *Book of the Dead*, which was to help the dead person before his judge, Osiris, when his heart was weighed on a scale; on the other end of the scale was placed the truth goddess Maat's ostrich feather. If the heart was heavier than the feather, the dead person was instantly devoured by the monster *Ammit*, whose head was a crocodile's and whose body was half lion and half hippopotamus. If his heart was lighter, Thoth declared him truthful and Horus carried him to the abode of the gods, presided over by Osiris, who was then incarnated by the dead man.

The religious ceremonies were supervised by priests. Most religious ceremonies corresponded to some natural event, and it was only on these occasions that the effigy of the god was presented to the people and carried about in processions, quite often on the Nile. The statue was not just the effigy of the god but his very essence.

ICONOGRAPHY

As far back as the beginning of the Old Kingdom, Egyptian art developed an iconography that remained basically unchanged for the next three thousand years, until the Roman occupation.

Let us examine first of all the four basic destinations of statues: officials' tombs, pharaohs' tombs, funerary temples, and ordinary temples. In order to go on living in the world beyond, the dead needed to have tombs as well as objects of daily use that would enable them to continue their activities. This is why the tombs of officials are filled with bas-reliefs or paintings representing religious and everyday scenes, scenes of country life and working life. These scenes would come alive when the priests uttered certain magic formulas during the funeral. The formulas also gave life to the statues of the dead person placed in the mastabas (tombs in the shape of a low, truncated pyramid), in a niche called *serdab* (in the rock-hewn tombs they were placed in a niche opening onto a room). The statues were to stand in for the body of the dead person, if by chance the body happened to become damaged by time or an accident. The dead therefore had to be identified either by statues or by images, and also by their names, inscribed in hieroglyphics on the base of the statues.

Pharaohs' tombs, on the other hand, contained mythical scenes of their life after death, which were illustrations of the holy books (*The Litanies of the Sun, The Book of the Opening of the Mouth, The Book of Hell, The Book of the Gates*). These tombs, too, contained niches in which statues were placed.

Inside the temples dedicated to the gods there were liturgical decorations; outside there were military scenes, but

Above: Small room in the temple of Ramesses II at Abu Simbel (1301–1235 B.C.), XIXth Dynasty. It shows the pharaoh between the gods Ptah, Amun, and Ra-Harakhty. Top: Colonnade of the temple of Amun at Luxor, XVIIIth–XIXth Dynasty (1504–1235 B.C.).

actually these were also connected to the cult, for all war booty belonged in effect to the gods. The statue of the god was placed in a chapel or sanctuary and every day it was fed, dressed, and decked out with jewels. Often access to the temple was by means of an avenue lined with sphinxes. Before the pylon entrance there were monumental statues or obelisks. Sometimes other statues were placed inside between the colonnades, as in Luxor or in the Ramesseum. The canon governing the art of sculpture was based on mathematical proportions but it also specified the appearance of the statue according to social class. In bas-reliefs and statuary the gods, the kings, and the officials were represented in the hieratical positions, either seated or walking. The king, who was Horus personified, was depicted as eternally youthful; his face was a portrait but his body followed the strict rules of the canon. Officials and priests made up the second social class. They, who could be approached by common mortals, were also represented in the hieratical positions, but their bodies were rendered realistically, like the plump "Sheikh el Beled" (see p. 37).

In the reliefs the scribes are usually shown in the walking hieratic position, but holding the pen and inkwell in their hands. In statuary, however, they are represented in their working position, sitting cross-legged with a roll of papyrus, the pen and inkwell in their hands.

There were no limitations imposed on the way the workers were represented, for in their case it was not the portrait but the activity that was important. Workers appear on reliefs decorating the tombs of officials but never those of kings, for kings had no contact with physical work. Statuettes called *ushabti* were also placed in the tombs; these were made of painted limestone and depicted such activities as making beer, woodworking, and so on.

Osirian pillars in the Ramesseum, the funerary temple of Ramesses II near Thebes (1301–1235 B.C.), XIXth Dynasty. The king is represented as Osiris.

179

The symbol of the unification of Upper and Lower Egypt is often found in official reliefs or statues of the New Kingdom; it is represented by two plants merging into one on top of a column.

During the New Kingdom the only iconographic innovation was the depiction of foreigners: on a fragment of relief from the temple of Thutmose III, for instance, we can see boatmen, whose brown bodies indicate that they were Nubians. Amenhotpe IV-Akhenaton attempted not only to break away from the polytheistic religion of Egypt but also to make the rules of the artistic canon obsolescent, by ordering artists to represent reality as they truly saw it. So the portraits of the king show him to have had an egg-shaped head, a thin neck, and a pot belly. Depicted in reliefs are scenes of his family life, including one, for example, in which the king, the queen and their daughters are shown eating roast duck (p. 185).

In Ptolemaic times, next to typically Egyptian scenes can be seen some in which the characters are dressed like Greeks (as in the tomb of Petosiris, at Tuna el Gebel, end of the fourth century B.C.). Among the statues of the gods are some relating to new cults (such as marble busts of Serapis and many effigies of Horus-Harpocrates). The numerous Greek artists working in Alexandria drew their inspiration from people who could be seen around the harbour: merchants, beggars, drunkards. There was quite a widespread use of erotic subjects based on local cults and these were often the subject of smaller pieces.

In the atrium of the temple of Edfu have been found small statues representing Leda and the Swan, but Leda has a typically Egyptian hair style.

For his statue in the temple at Karnak, Octavian posed in the hieratic position of the pharaohs. But the habit of clothing Egyptian gods and characters in the national costume of the

A hippopotamus hunt, coloured bas-relief from the tomb of Ti, at Saqqara, Vth Dynasty (2563–2423 B.C.).

dominating power continued in Roman times: we can see Anubis wearing a toga, or Horus and Thoth wearing a legionary's breastplate (necropolis of Kom el Shugafa).

A closer look should be given to capitals in Egyptian art. The first capitals were designed by Imhotep for King Zoser's funerary compound, and they were in the shape of an open lotus calix. Later capitals also sported papyrus flowers and palms. Capitals with their lotus petals closed (as they are during the night) adorned the hypostyle halls, while capitals with open flowers adorned the columns of the central nave. In the New Kingdom there appeared the so-called Hathorian capital, which consisted of the face of the goddess Hathor; but these were used only in temples dedicated to goddesses.

TECHNIQUE

As far back as the Old Kingdom the Egyptian artists worked according to a canon governing the rules of representing people in sculpture according to their social class; in addition, the human figure was depicted according to very rigorous mathematical proportions.

The first task of a sculptor working on a relief was to make up a model. He would divide a sheet of papyrus or a thin slab of stone into eighteen horizontal rows of equal squares. He then had to divide the proportions of the human figure to fit within the squares: there were two rows from the forehead to the base of the neck; ten from the neck to the knees, and six from the knees to the feet. The seated figure was allocated fourteen rows. The same proportions were applied to sculpture in the round, but there small plaster or stone models were used and the squares were marked on the back of the model. They were transferred onto the larger size by means of a system of points.

The material most commonly used in sculpture was stone, which was an easy commodity to find in Egypt: limestone, granite, alabaster, schists, and many others. After a rough sketch was made on the block of stone the statue was modelled by means of chisels and burins. Then its surface was smoothed with pumice stone or abrasive sand. Even hard stones such as black granite were sometimes painted in various colours. As for the relief, it was usually divided into a series of levels and finished off with the burin.

Wood was also often used, especially sycamore and ebony. The piece of wood was sketched on and chiselled. Various parts of the body, such as the arms, were usually modelled separately and fitted to the body with pegs. The finished surface was then covered with plaster and painted in several colours.

Metals such as bronze, copper alloy, and tin were less often used than stone or wood, mostly because of the scarcity of metals, which had to be imported from Cyprus and Nubia. The technique used for the large statues in more ancient times consisted of nailing hammered strips of metal onto a wooden base. The technique of cire-perdue was known as far back as Neolithic times but was used only for small statues. It consisted of making a model out of beeswax which was then covered by a mixture of clay and sand. After entry and exit holes were made in the model, it was placed in the furnace: the wax would then melt, leaving an empty space inside the model in which bronze could be poured. In later times the craftsmen used the technique of hollow casting, which allowed for much larger statues to be cast. There the model was first made of wax covering a clay base, and again covered in clay. After the clay was fired, melted bronze was poured in the space left empty by the melted wax. Terra cotta was used by Egyptian sculptors

The emperor Octavian Augustus dressed as a pharaoh (c. 30 B.C.). Cairo, Egyptian Museum.

only for smaller figures or models of ships or houses. The shape was modelled by the fingers and by means of thin wooden tools with one pointed and one flattened end. The colours were applied before the figures or models were fired.

FAMOUS SCULPTORS

We know the names of very few ancient Egyptian sculptors, and even if we can ascribe certain works to their workshops we cannot say for certain that they were made by their own hands.

The most ancient sculptor we know of is Nykainebty, who was in charge of the decoration of the mastaba of Ptahhotep II at Saqqara as head *gennty* (the *gennty* were sculptors who specialized in wood sculpture and bas-reliefs). Shen (XIIth Dynasty) was nother *gennty*; we owe to his workshop the reliefs and statues of Senwosret I at Abydos and Lisht. The portraits of Queen Tiy, wife of Amenhotpe III, and of princess Baketaton (in the Berlin museum) are attributed to the sculptor Iniuti (*c*.1400).

The name of Thutmose or Thutmes (*c*. 1350) was found inscribed on a piece of ivory in the place where the portraits of Queen Nafertiti were found. It is certain that many portraits of the Amarnian sovereigns came from his workshop, including the famous head of Akhenaton and that of Nafertiti in the Berlin museum. The sculptors Bek and Men also belonged to the same period. The latter, whose father also had been a sculptor, was the head of a workshop that specialized in the making and placing of colossal statues.

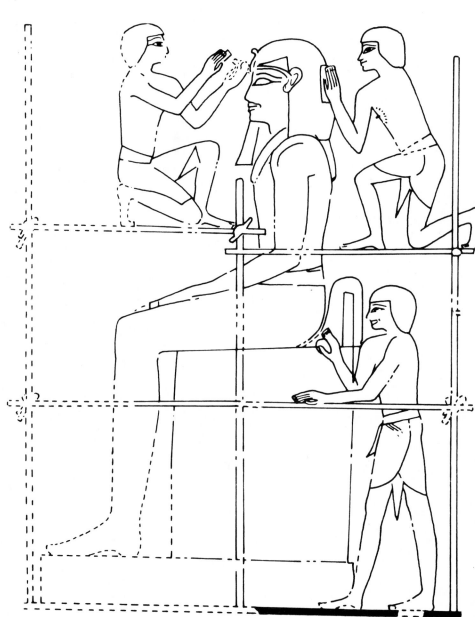

Above: The polishing and finishing of a statue. On page 183: Akhenaton kissing one of his daughters *(1372–1354* B.C.*), XVIIIth Dynasty. This unfinished statue was found in a sculptor's workshop at Tell el 'Amarna.*

THE REDISCOVERY OF EGYPT

By the time of the Roman occupation of Egypt the Egyptians had only a vague and fragmentary idea of their past history, and in fact were no longer able to read the hieroglyphic writing. The word itself is significant in this respect: it comes from the Greek *hieros*, "sacred," and *glyphein*, "to write," while we know today that the so-called hieroglyphs dealt with all subjects, not just sacred texts. The priests (the most learned people) considered them philosophical symbols. When Herodotus, the Greek historian of the end of the sixth century B.C., visited Egypt, many of the ancient monuments were already covered up, deep in sand.

Later the Western world knew of Egypt mostly through the Bible: the Pyramids, for instance, were thought to be the granaries of Joseph, Jacob's son.

It was not until 1798, the year of Napoleon Bonaparte's expedition, that new light was shed on Egypt's past, for the expedition included numerous archeologists and experts in all subjects.

The results of their observations and researches were reported in the famous *Description de l'Egypte*, which describes the country from artistic, zoological, geographical, hydrographical, botanic and ethnographic points of view. The most striking figure of the expedition was that of Dominique Vivant Denon, who went down to the First Cataract of the Nile, making sketches and notes on everything he saw. Back in Paris, he published an account of his journey, *Voyage dans la Basse et Haute-Egypte* (1802).

Bonaparte's expedition started a new fashion in France, a style called *retour d'Egypte*, which drew its inspiration from Egyptian art; with the new fascination for things exotic this could not but attract the taste of the "neoclassical" generation which hitherto had been drawing inspiration mostly from ancient Greece. So the Egyptian style was

added to the neoclassical decorative repertoire and is evident in the proliferation of sphinxes, furniture decoration, dress, and winged suns.

We owe the deciphering of the hieroglyphs to Jean-François Champollion (1790–1832). Despite other people's opinions and the tradition hitherto maintained, Champollion discovered, between 1824 and 1828, that hieroglyphs were phonetic symbols transformed into simple signs in the hieratic writing and even simpler signs in the demotic writing.

His discovery was based mostly on a trilingual (Greek, Demotic, Hieroglyphic) stela found at Rosetta, in the Nile Delta, during the Bonaparte expedition. Champollion first deciphered the names Ptolemy and Cleopatra. Later, with the contribution of other scholars, the hieroglyphs became totally accessible.

At the same time archeological excavations and discoveries were taking place. Auguste Mariette was the first to organize a systematic archeological exploration of Egypt; he also founded the Cairo Museum in 1863. Gaston Maspéro discovered the necropolis of Deir el Bahri. The German archeologist Richard Lepsius, who is considered to be the father of Egyptology, made digs at Memphis, Thebes, and Tell el 'Amarna from 1843 to 1845. William F. Petrie worked in Egypt from 1880 to 1926, studying the construction of the Pyramids and many other aspects of Egyptian technique and daily life.

The twentieth century saw the work of archeologists of all nations. Among them must be mentioned Howard Carter, who in 1922 discovered the tomb of Tutankhamun, the last unprofaned tomb of the Valley of the Kings, which for that very reason proved to be a source of unique documentation. Among recent excavations is the one that brought to light the temple of Thutmose III at Deir el Bahri; this was the work of the Polish archeological mission headed by Kazimierz Michalowski.

GUIDE TO THE MONUMENTS

From north to south the following groups of monuments, or single monuments, can be found:

TANIS: remains of four colossal statues in the temple of Ramesses II (XIXth Dynasty).

MEMPHIS: colossal statue of Ramesses II, one of the few things remaining from the temple of Ptah.

GIZA: pyramids of Cheops, Chephren, and Mycerinus (IVth Dynasty); sphinx with the face of Chephren; reliefs decorating the mastabas and rock-hewn tombs in the neighbourhood (Old Kingdom).

ABU SIR: reliefs of the funerary temple of Pharaoh Sahura (Vth Dynasty).

SAQQARA: great compound around the pyramid (the first ever built, work of the architect Imhotep) and the funerary temple of Zoser (IIIrd Dynasty); temple of Wenis (Vth Dynasty); mastabas (all from the Old Kingdom); and funerary compound of Pharaoh Pepy II.

DAHSHUR: reliefs in the funerary temple of Snefru (IVth Dynasty).

TELL EL 'AMARNA: painted decorations in the rock-hewn tombs of courtiers; reliefs in the tomb of Amenhotpe IV-Akhenaton (XVIIIth Dynasty).

ABYDOS: reliefs in the funerary temple of Sety I (XIXth Dynasty).

DENDERA: reliefs and *Mammisi* (Birth Sanctuary) in the temple of the goddess Hathor (XXXth Dynasty, under Nektanebo I, 378–360 B.C.).

Above: Measuring the sphinx; from the Voyage *of Vivant Denon. Top: Funerary stela inscribed with hieroglyphics, XVIIIth Dynasty (1580–1314 B.C.). Florence, Museo Archeologico.*

KARNAK: reliefs and statues in the temple compound of Amun.

LUXOR: reliefs and statues in the temple of Amun, linked with the preceding temple by an avenue lined with sphinxes.

Necropolises on the left bank of the Nile: reliefs in the Ramesseum (funerary temple of Ramesses II, XIXth Dynasty). Colossi of Memnon (portraits of Amenhotpe III, XVIIIth Dynasty), only remains on the surface of the king's funerary temple. Reliefs in the funerary temple of Ramesses III (XXth Dynasty) at Medinet Habu. Reliefs in the funerary temple of Mentuhotpe (XIth Dynasty) and Hatshepsut (XVIIIth Dynasty) at Deir el Bahri. Valley of the Kings (in Arabic, Biban el Muluk). Reliefs in the tombs of kings, including Tutankhamun's (XVIIIth Dynasty) and Sety I's (XIXth Dynasty).

EDFU: reliefs in the temple of Horus (Ptolemaic period).

ASWAN: granite quarries with some unfinished monuments, interesting for the study of technique.

ELEPHANTINE: reliefs in the necropolis of local princes.

PHILAE: reliefs in the temple of Isis (Greco-Roman period).

ABU SIMBEL: colossal statues and reliefs in the rock-hewn temple of Ramesses II (XIXth Dynasty) dedicated to Ra-Harakhty, Amun, Ptah, and the king himself. Colossal statues and decoration of the temple dedicated by Ramesses II to the goddess Hathor.

To make possible both the construction of the Aswan Dam and the preservation of the most precious monuments, which would have been submerged otherwise, archeological expeditions were organized from every part of the world, under the auspices of UNESCO and with the cooperation of the Egyptian and Sudanese governments. As a result, the temples of Kalabshah, Amada, Abu Simbel, Tafeh and Dabod were dismantled and transferred to higher ground.

MUSEUMS

BERLIN: *Staatliche Museen, Ägyptische Abteilung.* Collection started in the eighteenth century and enriched in the mid-nineteenth century by R. Lepsius's expedition, and by further additions. Works from the Old and New Kingdoms (heads of queens Tiy and Nafertiti).

BOSTON: *Museum of Fine Arts.* The Egyptian section was established at the end of the nineteenth century and consists mainly of bequests. Objects from the tomb of Thutmose IV. Objects discovered at the foot of the great pyramid of Giza. Sculptures from the Old Kingdom (King Mycerinus and Queen Khamerernebti).

CAIRO: *Egyptian Museum.* Founded in 1863 by the archeologist Auguste Mariette, it is the most complete Egyptian museum in the world. Constantly enriched by new archeological finds. Among the most famous statues: *Pharaoh Zoser,* and *Rahotep and Nofret.* Among the reliefs: the *tablet of Narmer,* the wooden reliefs of Hesyra's tomb. Sarcophagi; treasure of Tutankhamun.

VATICAN CITY: *Musei Vaticani (Museo Gregoriano Egizio).* Founded in 1836 by Gregory XVI, it contains mostly objects collected by Pius VI and Pius VII (colossal statues of the goddess Sachis), and objects discovered in Rome (statue of Tui, mother of Ramesses II).

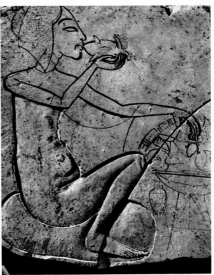

Above: An Amarna princess *(1372–1354* B.C.*), XVIIIth Dynasty. Cairo, Egyptian Museum. Top:* The Mammisi, *at Dendera, was the "Birth Sanctuary" of the goddess Hathor.*

185

COPENHAGEN: *Ny Carlsberg Glyptotek*. The Egyptian section was formed in the early twentieth century from a bequest of the bishop of Sjaelland. *Ramesses II and Ptah*, from Memphis; statue of *Geb*, from Karnak; *Anubis enthroned*, from Luxor; *Scribe* (end of the XVIIIth Dynasty).

FLORENCE: *Museo Egiziano*. Formed in 1855 from the Nizzoli collection originally acquired in 1824, and from objects brought back from the Tuscan expedition to Egypt under the direction of Ippolito Rosellini (1828–1829). In 1880 it became part of the new *Museo Archeologico* (founded in 1870) and was further enriched by the findings of Ernesto Schiapparelli (1885, 1891–1892). The most important museum in Italy, after the Turin museum, for things Egyptian.

LONDON: *British Museum*. The Egyptian section, which dates from the mid-eighteenth century, was enriched after the British victory over the French in Egypt (1801). Sarcophagi, the Rosetta Stone.

NEW YORK: *Metropolitan Museum of Art*. The Egyptian section contains the statue of *Queen Hatshepsut* and the *Sphinx of Senwosret III*.

PARIS: *Louvre*. The Egyptian collection was formed with works brought back from Bonaparte's expedition in Egypt by Baron Vivant Denon, director of the museum for almost twenty years. Reliefs, sarcophagi, ornaments, jewelry, statues, including the *Scribe* from Saqqara, the gold, silver and bronze *Queen Karomama*, the *Woman bearing offerings* in wood, and the granite *God Amun*.

TURIN: *Museo Egizio*. Originally formed by the collection of B. Drovetti, French consul general in Egypt, bought by Carlo Felice in 1824. To this were added objects brought back by, among other people, E. Schiapparelli in the early twentieth century and G. Farina (1930–1937) from the Valley of the Queens, Deir el Medineh, Giza, Heliopolis, and the necropolises of Ashmunein, Aswan, Tuna el Gebel, and Hammamia. Sarcophagi, ornaments, many statues, including the granite statues of Thutmose I, Ramesses II, Haremhab, his wife Mutnodjmet, and the goddess Sakhmet.

Scribes (14th century B.C.*), XVIIIth Dynasty. From Tell el 'Amarna (?). Florence, Museo Archeologico.*

BIBLIOGRAPHY

Adriani, A. *Repertorio d'arte dell'Egitto Greco-Romano*, Palermo, 1961, 2 vols.

Aldred, C. *Old Kingdom Art in Ancient Egypt*, London, 1949.
Middle Kingdom Art in Ancient Egypt, London, 1950.
New Kingdom Art in Ancient Egypt, London, 1951.

Baumgartel, E. J. *The Cultures of Prehistoric Egypt*, Oxford, 1955.

Bille-De Mot, E. *Die Revolution des Pharao Echnaton*, Munich, 1965.

Bissing, F. *Ägyptische Kunstgeschichte*, Berlin, 1934–1935.

Bosticco, S. *Stele egiziane, Museo Archeologico di Firenze*, Rome, 1959.

Bothmer, B. V. *Egyptian Sculpture of the Late Period*, Brooklyn Museum, 1960.

Breccia, E. *Alexandrea ad Aegyptum*, Bergamo, 1922.

Cambridge Ancient History, Cambridge, 1961–1965, new edition (vols. 1–2).

Capart J. *Les débuts de l'art en Egypte*, Brussels, 1904.
L'art égyptien. Choix de documents, Brussels, 1922–1947, 4 vols. (vol. II, *Statuaire*; vol. IV, *Arts mineurs*).
Documents pour servir à l'étude de l'art égyptien, Paris, 1927–1931, 2 vols.

Christophe, L. A. *Abou-Simbel*, Brussels, 1965.

Daumas, F. *La civilisation de l'Egypte pharaonique*, Paris, 1965.

Desroches-Noblecourt, Ch. *Le style égyptien*, Paris, 1946.
L'ancienne Egypte, l'extraordinaire aventure amarnienne, Paris, 1960.
L'art égyptien, Paris, 1961.
Toutankhamon et son temps, Paris, 1967.

Donadoni, S. *Arte egizia*, Turin, 1955.
Storia della letteratura egiziana antica, Milan, 1957.

Du Bourguet, P., and E. Drioton, *Les pharaons à la conquête de l'art*, Paris, 1965.

Erman, A., and H. Ranke, *Ägypten und ägyptisches Leben im Altertum*, Tubingen, 1923.

Fechheimer, H. *Die Plastik der Ägypter*, Berlin, 1914.

Gardiner, A. H. *Ancient Egyptian Onomastica*, Oxford, 1947, 3 vols.

Hayes, W. C. *Most Ancient Egypt*, University of Chicago, 1964.

Iversen, E. *Canon and Proportions in Egyptian Art*, London, 1955.

Lange, K., and M. Hirmer, *Ägypten. Architektur, Plastik, Malerei in Drei Jahrtausenden*, Munich, 1967.

Leclant, J. *Dans les pays des pharaons*, Paris, 1958.

Lefebvre, G. *Le tombeau de Petosiris*, Cairo, 1924.

Lepsius, R. *Denkmäler aus Ägypten und Äthiopien*, Berlin, 1849–1859, 12 vols.
Texte, Leipzig, 1897–1913, 5 vols.
Ergänzungsband, 1913.

Lucas, A. *Ancient Egyptian Materials and Industries*, London, 1947.

Michalowski, K. *Faras, centre artistique de la Nubie chrétienne*, Leyden, 1966.
L'art de l'ancienne Egypte, Paris, 1968.

Montecchi, A. *Un impero scomparso*, Milan, 1957.

Montet, P. *Les scènes de la vie privée dans les tombeaux égyptiens de l'Ancien Empire*, Strasbourg, 1925.

Mysliwiec, K. *Le Portrait royal dans le bas-relief du Nouvel Empire*, Warsaw, 1976 (Travaux du Centre d'Archéologie Méditerranéenne de l'Académie Polonaise des Sciences).

Pirenne, J. *Histoire de la civilisation de l'Egypte ancienne*, Neuchâtel, 1961–1963, 3 vols.

Porter, B., and R. Moss, *Topographical Bibliography of Ancient Egyptian Hieroglyphic Texts, Reliefs and Paintings*, Oxford, 1927–1964, 7 vols.

Posener, G. (with S. Sauneron and J. Yoyotte), *Dictionnaire de la civilisation égyptienne*, Paris, 1959.

Rosellini, I. *I monumenti dell'Egitto e della Nubia*, Pisa, 1832 (*Monumenti storici*), 1834 (*Monumenti civili*).

Scamuzzi, E. *Museo Egizio di Torino*, Turin, 1963.

Schäfer, H. *Von Ägyptischer Kunst*, Wiesbaden, 1963, 3rd ed.

Selim Hassan, *Le Sphinx*, Cairo, 1951.

Shinnie, P. L. *Méroé, A Civilization of the Sudan*, London, 1967.

Smith, W. S. *Art and Architecture in Ancient Egypt*, London, 1958 (Pelican History of Art).

Vandier, J. *La sculpture égyptienne*, Paris, 1951.
Manuel d'archéologie égyptienne, Paris, 1952–1958, 3 vols.

Vigneau, A., and E. Drioton, *Le Musée du Caire*, Paris, 1949 (Encyclopédie Photographique de l'Art).

Werbruck, M. *Le temple d'Hatshepsut à Deir el-Bahari*, Brussels, 1949.

Wilson, J. *L'Egypte, vie et mort d'une civilisation*, Paris, 1961.

Woldering, I. *Ägypten*, Baden-Baden, 1962.

INDEX

PHOTOGRAPHIC SOURCES

The abbreviations t, b, r, l refer to the position of the illustration on the page (top, bottom, right, left)

© B. Arthaud Editeur
(L'Egypte, by L. Cottrell, Grenoble)
103, 178

Ashmolean Museum, Oxford
80l, 80r, 81r, 82

Maurice Babey, Basle
38, 53

Bildarchiv Preussicher Kulturbesitz, West Berlin
146t

Boudot-Lamotte, Paris
29

British Museum, London
129, 130

Brooklyn Museum, New York
108l, 108r, 151

Bulloz, Paris
185

Farabola-Alinari, Milan
66, 146b

Istituto Geografico de Agostini, Novara
185

Kodansha Ltd., Tokyo
40, 41, 48, 49, 57, 63, 81l, 88l, 124, 172r

Kopperman, Munich
164

© Editions d'art Lucien Mazenod, L'art de l'ancienne Egypte, by K. Michalowski, Paris. Drawing by Halina Lewak, Warsaw
72

Photo Jean Vertut, Paris
180, 181

Metropolitan Museum of Art, New York
91, 116, 117, 119l, 131

Kazimierz Michalowski, Warsaw
24

Museum of Fine Arts, Boston
97, 126

© Newsweek, New York: photo John G. Ross, Rome
46, 175

Ny Carlsberg Glyptotek, Copenhagen
83, 174

Takashi Okamura, Rome
30, 85, 113, 154, 156

François René Roland, Paris
2, 13, 33, 34, 35, 36, 37, 39, 42, 43, 45, 47, 50, 51, 52, 54, 55, 56, 58, 59, 60, 61, 62, 64, 65, 84, 86l, 86r, 87, 88r, 89, 90, 92, 93, 94, 95, 96, 98, 99, 100l, 100r, 101, 102, 104, 105, 106, 107, 109, 110, 111, 112, 114, 115, 118, 119r, 120, 121, 122, 123, 125, 127, 128, 133, 135, 136, 137, 140, 141, 142, 143, 145, 147, 148, 149, 150, 152, 153, 155, 157, 158, 159, 160–161, 162, 165, 166, 167, 168, 169, 170, 171, 172l.

C. Rosso, Turin
134, 173

Staatliche Museen, Berlin
4, 6, 132, 144

Henri Stierlin, Geneva
163

A. Vigneau, Paris
183

Archivio Arnoldo Mondadori Editore, Milan
44, 177, 178, 179, 184, 186

We should like to express our thanks to Signor Giorgio Lise, Civica Raccolta Stampe A. Bertarelli, Milan.